INDIA'S GATEWAY:

Gujarat, Mumbai & Britain   Tim Smith

The India's Gateway exhibition and book are sponsored by Prashad.

The India's Gateway project is supported using public funding by the National Lottery through Arts Council England.

The India's Gateway exhibition and book were produced by Tim Smith, Elizabeth Smith, and Champak Limbachia of Oriental Arts. Audience development and evaluation by Kate Wafer of Wafer Hadley.

Additional research in Gujarat by Niti Acharya and Gerard Greene was funded by a British Council 'Connections Through Culture' grant.

First published in the UK in 2016 by

Northern Arts Publications
Red Doles Lane
Huddersfield
West Yorkshire HD2 1YE

www.dandmheritage.co.uk

ISBN: 978-1-911148-04-3

Artwork production and print: Northern Arts Publications.

Photo right: Ashok Makwana with yarn hung out to dry in a dye workshop in Bagasara. This family business is based in the yard of their home and is part of the Udyog Bharti khadi co-operative.

PAKISTAN

RAJASTHAN

GUJARAT

Bhuj

Sukhpar
● Madhapur
● Baladia
● Melomora

Mandvi ●

GANDHINAGAR ◉

● Adalaj

Ahmedabad

GULF OF KUTCH

Morbi ●

Vadtal ●

Anand ●

Vadodara

Dwarka ●

Jamnagar

Rajkot

MADHYA
PRADESH

Gondal ●

Virpur ●

Bhavnagar

Bharuch

Porbandar

Amreli ●

Palitana

Junagadh

Bagasara ●

Jambur ●

Surat

Lajpur ● ● Baleshwar

Veraval ●

Navsari

Diu

Dandi ● ● Pipaldara
Gadat ●
● Alipor
● Chikhli
● Valsad

Daman ●

MAHARASHTRA

Mumbai ●

ARABIAN SEA

DADRA & NAGAR HAVELI

iv

Gujarat State

Modern day Gujarat is roughly the same size as Britain, with a population of just over 60 million people. Although most of Gujarat is flat, the landscape itself is varied, ranging from the salt deserts of the north to the fertile agricultural plains of the south.

Gujaratis have very diverse lifestyles, but over 90% of them speak Gujarati as their mother tongue, with the remainder of people using Kutchi, Urdu, Marathi and English as their first language. Hindi, the national language of India, is widely spoken. Gujarat's capital city is Gandhinagar, while its largest city is Ahmedabad.

Gujarat has the longest coastline of any state in India. The coast runs along the Arabian Sea, and is dotted with ancient ports that have a history of trade with the Arab world going back over 3,000 years.

The present day state of Gujarat came into existence in 1960. Under British rule the region lay within Bombay Presidency, and on Independence in 1947 it became part of Bombay State. In 1960 Bombay State was redrawn and the southern areas, including the city of Bombay, became part of Maharashtra. Then in 1996 Bombay was renamed Mumbai after the Hindu goddess Mumbadevi, the city's presiding deity.

The vast majority of British Gujaratis originate from the coastal belt, which runs from Kutch in the north to the southern areas towards Mumbai. Different areas of Gujarat often have links to specific towns or cities in Britain, and many of these places are featured in this book. The locations where the photographs were taken are marked on the map opposite.

People of Gujarati heritage make up around half of the 1.5 million Indians and British Indians now living in Britain, the country's biggest ethnic minority.

Introduction

'There's a little bit of India in everyone who lives in Britain. I wish more people realised that.'

These heartfelt words were said to me by a British Indian friend in Yorkshire and referred to everyone who lives here, British Indian or otherwise. His remark set me thinking about my own connections with India and how they led to the photographs in this book. Sometimes these connections have been part of my working life as a photographer, and sometimes they've popped up in places I least expected them to. Like Dolphin Street in Newport, South Wales.

I moved into one of the two-up, two-down terrace houses in Dolphin Street in 1982 because the rent was cheap, and I was studying photography at the local art college. While I was excited about my course, I was initially unimpressed with my new surroundings, close to the muddy River Usk flowing brown towards the docks. But it was the best move I ever made. The docklands were filled with rows of ordinary terraced streets like mine: but inside those houses were people with extraordinary life stories, connecting Newport to the rest of the world. I began to explore the ways in which these people's lives had brought them to Britain from all over the world, and this became the focus of much of my work as a photographer.

Left: *A textile shop in Willingdon Crescent in Jamnagar.*

Above: *A view of Dolphin Street from the local primary school, 1984.*

The owner of a café and boarding house catering for sailors in the docklands area of Newport, 1983.

In Newport the link to the world was coal. During the age of steam Welsh coal had fuelled British ships carrying cargo all over the world, and these ships recruited their crews in Kingston and Karachi, Aden and Bombay. For a long time Welsh coal was also Newport's most valuable export. Most of it ended up stockpiled in Aden, a deep-water harbour on the coast of Yemen where British steamships would stop to refuel on their way to Bombay, Britain's main maritime link with India. (With an extraordinary piece of imperial map-making the British even made

Aden part of British India – ruled over and paid for by the government in Bombay.) British ships took on experienced Arab and Indian sailors from communities who had been travelling the trade routes of the Indian Ocean for hundreds of years – Yemenis from Aden, and Indians from Bombay and ancient Gujarati ports like Mandvi, Surat and Porbandar.

Once the British boats arrived back at ports like Newport, their Arab and Indian crews came ashore as cargoes were transferred or they looked for a new

ship to work on. The crews stayed in local boarding houses and ate in cafes that had begun to serve some of Britain's first Arab and Asian cuisine. Some sailors found jobs in the docklands, settled and sent for their families to join them: a pattern repeated around Britain. My neighbours in Dolphin Street included Indian and Yemeni families, people from the Caribbean, Pakistan, Bangladesh, Mauritius and China, and 'locals' from England, Ireland, Scotland and Wales. I started taking photos up and down the street: in the school, the pub, and in the café run by a former sailor. I was invited (and sometimes invited myself) to weddings, birthdays and barbeques. I learned that getting access to the rituals of ordinary life could offer extraordinary opportunities for making photographs.

I finished college in 1984 with a set of pictures of Dolphin Street that became my first ever exhibition, shown at the Commonwealth Institute in London. The same photographs landed me my first job, for the Bradford Heritage Recording Unit, which used photography and spoken history to explore and document the lives of local people. Like Newport, Bradford had strong links with the Indian subcontinent, particularly to Bombay and the Gujarat region. This time the link was textiles. Bradford is a city that boomed during the Industrial Revolution, growing from a small market town to the woollen textile capital of the world. And many of the designs and techniques that informed the growth of British textiles were copied from Gujarat's ancient and hugely influential textile industry.

It was not only ideas and technology that forged close connections between Britain and India, but the migration of people too. When Britain needed labour to work in its factories after the Second World War, it recruited workers from areas like Gujarat and Punjab, which already had particularly close links with Britain. Gujarat has a long tradition of overseas trade and migration, and large numbers of people made the journey from there to Britain, including many professional and business people. By the 1960s large Gujarati communities had formed in Manchester, Lancashire, Yorkshire, the Midlands and in Greater London. The communities grew further in the early 1970s with the arrival of East African Asians of Gujarati descent who had been forced to leave their homes in countries such as Uganda, Kenya, Tanzania and Malawi.

Ever since I lived in Newport my work has explored stories around migration, culture and identity and over the past three decades I've photographed many of the British Asian communities across the UK. I'm fascinated by individual life stories that often depend on chance and circumstance, but are also shaped by the impact of world events: whether it be the arrival of British ships on Indian shores over 400 years ago, the role of the Indian army in the First and Second World Wars, or the Partition of India in 1947. The ambition of much of my work is to weave together these historical narratives with personal stories.

With India's Gateway I wanted to tell these stories from the other end. By travelling back along the lines of migration to modern-day Gujarat and Mumbai, I wanted to take photographs and gather stories that explored the shared history between Britain and India, much of which is still visible today. For me, India's Gateway reflects Gujarat and Mumbai's vibrant diversity of cultures, and reveals glimpses of everyday life acted out against a landscape shaped by the region's rich history of trade, seafaring and migration.

Before setting off to India I travelled around England asking British Gujaratis for advice about where to go and who to meet in Gujarat. I found that different towns and cities in Britain have links to very specific places in Gujarat, and I planned my journey to reflect this. I'm very grateful for the help and advice I received, which shaped both the overall project and the photographs in this book.

I travelled to Gujarat in 2014, spending time in Mumbai and then heading northwards, covering over 3,000 miles through Gujarat state. I timed my visit to coincide with the so-called 'NRI season,' when many Non-Resident Indians (NRIs) escape the cold British winter to visit their family homes. This enabled me to meet, photograph and interview lots of people from Britain, as well as hundreds of Indians with family and business connections to the UK. Sometimes these meetings were arranged in advance, and conversations begun in Bradford, London or Leicester were continued in Navsari, Rajkot or Porbandar. At other times they happened by chance, just going into a shop or getting into a lift. By seeking out places that I knew had strong links with Britain it was relatively easy to meet people. Occasionally I would overhear a British regional accent and start a conversation. Usually

Celebrating Navratri at the Shree Prajapati Mandir in Bradford, 1987.

as a photographer I try to remain unnoticed but sometimes being the only white person for miles around had its advantages, as people who were often 'Britishers' themselves would ask me where I was from, and go on to share invaluable insights into their own lives. And then they'd often pass me on to friends and family further down the road.

India's Gateway is the result of a personal journey, but one that was guided by a huge number of people. I hope the images and stories in this book will resonate for many readers by reflecting aspects of their own lives, as well as giving people an insight into how our shared histories have put 'a little bit of India in everyone who lives in Britain,' and have left a little bit of Britain in India too.

Tim Smith

Gujarat & Trade

Gujarat has been a centre for international trade for over 3,000 years. Its coastline along the Arabian Sea is studded with ports, which connected northern India with the outside world and the region became the crossroads for sea routes between Arabia, Africa, south-east Asia, Indonesia, and China.

This seafaring network was dominated by Gujarati, Arab and Chinese sailors and traders. Control of the region's ports and trading routes made local kingdoms very wealthy. People from Gujarat travelled widely and settled in many parts of the world from East Africa to the Pacific Ocean. Trade also brought people from overseas and from other parts of Asia to Gujarat. The region has a long history of being home to a diverse range of people and has many distinct communities.

The port of Bombay grew from a small settlement on one of a string of seven islands to the most important commercial centre in the region, a focus for British control and later for the Indian Independence movement. In 1996 the city's name was formally changed to Mumbai.

Sea trading and shipbuilding traditionally go hand in hand. Craftsmen on the coast of Gujarat still build

Left: A boat builder climbing up the hull of a dhow under construction in Mandvi.

the traditional dhows that were used for centuries by Indian and Arab traders to ferry their goods along the ancient sea routes. The skills and tools these shipbuilders use today resemble those used to make the ships that first brought Dutch, Portuguese and English traders to India.

In Gujarat the shipwrights use basic hand tools to cut and shape hardwood planks, once sourced locally but now imported from south-east Asia. The dhows they build are valued for their durability and their shape and size, which allow them access to shallow water harbours. Originally dhows were sailboats, requiring their crew to have expert knowledge of the changing ocean currents and winds that shifted direction depending on the season. These days engines have replaced the sails.

The large boats have a capacity of 2,000 tons of cargo, and take 15 men three years to build, at a cost of between two and three-crore rupees, £200,000 to £300,000. Global sea trade is now dominated by huge container ships that need large deep-sea harbours like Mumbai, which is India's busiest commercial port. Most of the boats now built in Gujarat are smaller versions used for fishing. This could be the last generation of shipbuilders using ancient skills to build large wooden cargo boats. Today only a few craftsmen still have work, and the boats they build are nearly all commissioned by wealthy buyers from the Arab world.

Above: Fishing boats in dry dock at Vanakbara, a busy port on Diu Island.

Right: People feeding fish and hawkers selling fish-food along the promenade in Dwarka. This is India's most westerly town, situated on the tip of Gujarat's Kathiawad peninsula, which juts out into the Arabian Sea.

Above: Retired sailors in Mota Salaya, part of the ancient port of Mandvi and home to around 250 former seamen. Second from left is Ismali Bhatti, aged 72, who travelled all over the world as a sailor for Ellerman Lines, a Liverpool based shipping company.

Left: Teams of carpenters building fishing boats in Vanakbara on Diu Island. Gujarat is one of India's most important sources of fish and seafood.

Above: Repairing an ocean-going cargo vessel in Porbandar, which was once one of the most important international ports along Gujarat's coast. Nowadays most of the region's cargo is handled through Mumbai.

Right: A huge cargo boat, or dhow, being built in Mandvi. Dhows are built entirely of wood by craftsmen using hand tools to a traditional design unchanged for hundreds of years.

Above: *Unloading the catch at Andheri Beach in Mumbai. The area's original inhabitants were fishermen, but pollution and overfishing by trawlers now threaten their livelihood.*

Left: *A woman shelling prawns with her baby at Sassoon Dock. The dock was built as Mumbai's first cotton trading harbour and is now a busy fishing port and wholesale seafood market.*

THE HINDU COMMUNITIES

Around 90% of Gujaratis are Hindus. The religion is rooted in the Indian subcontinent and evolved over several thousand years. Because of these ancient origins, Hindu traditions across India embrace a very wide range of beliefs and practices. Some traditions are recognised by only a few villages, others are popular right across the subcontinent and in places where Hindus have settled overseas.

Perhaps the greatest degree of shared belief concerns the authority of the Vedas, the oldest of the sacred texts on which Hinduism is based. Many of these texts are in Sanskrit, an ancient literary language that was also used as a common language across India. Sanskrit is still widely used as the sacred language of Hinduism.

In most Hindu homes a chosen deity is worshipped daily. Outside the home worship takes place in temples and consists of puja, sometimes a simple act of prayer, but often a complex set of rituals. Like many other places in India, Gujarat has a wealth of pilgrimage sites. Many sites are devoted to specific deities or traditions within Hindu teaching, and remain important places of pilgrimage for British Indians visiting from abroad.

Between half and three-quarters of the Hindu communities in Britain are of Gujarati origin.

Above & left: The Shree Swaminarayan Mandir, which dominates the small town of Vadtal.

Above & left: *Visitors to the Shree Swaminarayan Mandir in Vadtal. Swaminarayan (1781–1830) was a hugely popular teacher, and the Mandir is an important place of pilgrimage for Hindus who follow his teachings.*

THE JAIN COMMUNITIES

Although Jains make up less than one per cent of the population of India, their community has been very influential for more than 2,500 years. Jainism has similarities to Hinduism, with a shared respect for nature and nonviolence, and the number of Jains has declined as some have converted to Hinduism.

Jains are found working as merchants and traders all over India, but a very large proportion of them live in Gujarat. As many Jains avoid using public transport, white-robed figures, often barefoot, can frequently be seen walking along the roadsides in Gujarat.

At the pilgrimage site of Shatrunjaya, near Palitana, more than 900 temples crown the summit of a pair of hills. Each temple enclosure is named after the merchant who funded it. A young Jain man at Shatrunjaya explained:

Many of the Jains were wealthy traders and merchants, and they would use their wealth for philanthropic acts such as building temples. The temples here were built by such people. There are many others all over India but this is the most popular site.

There were many Jains in places like Ahmedabad and Surat, doing trade with the Arabs who were just across the sea, and then the British arrived in Surat so we did trade with them too. I'm a student and I've travelled here on a kind of pilgrimage from Bombay, where there's a big Jain community. As well as the religious aspects, the temple complexes are important as they first provide work for people building them, and eventually the area becomes a centre for trade and commerce.'

Left & right: Jain pilgrims at the complex of temples scattered across the two holy hills of Shatrunjaya near Palitana, India's most important Jain site.

THE MUSLIM COMMUNITIES

Nearly ten per cent of Gujaratis are Muslims. Islam arrived in Gujarat as soon as it had spread through the Arab world, brought to India by Arab and Persian traders who formed settlements on the coast as early as the eighth century. Many of these men married local women, and over time adopted the local Gujarati language and culture.

Much more significant was the thirteenth century invasion of north-west India by Muslim armies from central Asia. This resulted in the colonisation of parts of northern India, with Muslim rulers establishing themselves in Delhi. The Delhi Sultanate marks a key point in Indian history, the beginning of five centuries of Muslim rule in northern India, with Delhi becoming the region's most important city.

The Mughals were the most famous of India's Muslim rulers; their courts were based in Delhi, Lahore and Agra. From these centres of wealth and power the Mughal Empire governed much of northern and central India until the early eighteenth century. Gujarat became part of the Mughal Empire after the Mughal Emperor Akbar conquered it in the 1570s.

During this time Surat became the principal port in India, linking the Mughal Empire with the outside world as well as being the main port from which Muslims set off from India to make the pilgrimage to Mecca. Surat became internationally famous as the place to do business with the wealthy Mughal Empire and thus became an early base for the first Europeans who arrived seeking to become part of the lucrative trading networks of the Indian Ocean.

Surat and other Gujarati ports attracted sailors and business people from many different parts of the world, many of them Muslims, who settled in the region but continued their traditional occupations of seafaring and trading. Some local people also converted to Islam. Today Muslims are the largest religious group in Gujarat after the Hindus and many of the largest communities can still be found in coastal towns and cities where their ancestors first arrived.

Left: A mosque in Kera near Bhuj, which was renovated with funds from the World Federation of Khoja Shia Ithna-Asheri Muslim Communities, whose headquarters is in London.

Right: A man sweeps the central courtyard of the Jama Masjid in Ahmedabad. Sultan Ahmed Shah, ruler of the Gujarat Sultanate who gave his name to the city of Ahmedabad, completed the mosque in 1424.

Above: A man and his granddaughter outside their house in Kera near Bhuj.

Left: A man cleaning the prayer hall of the Jama Masjid in Ahmedabad.

Above: Visitors at the popular tomb of Haji Ali, which was built on an island off the coast of Mumbai and can be reached only at low tide. Haji Ali is said to have given away all his possessions before setting out on a pilgrimage to Mecca, but he died on the journey and his body floated back to Mumbai in a casket.

Right: A young man scatters petals over graves in a Muslim shrine by the river Tapi in Surat. Surat was once India's busiest port and the departure point for Muslims going on pilgrimage to Mecca.

THE PARSI COMMUNITIES

The Parsis are the descendants of refugees from Persia (now Iran) who emigrated to India just over 1,000 years ago. They are followers of the Iranian religious philosopher Zoroaster, whose ideas led to the formation of the Zoroastrian religion around the sixth century BCE.

According to tradition, Parsis set sail for India to escape religious persecution in their homeland. They settled in southern Gujarat, where they established small communities of farmers, weavers and carpenters in towns such as Surat and Navsari.

Some Parsis brokered trade between local Indians and the Portuguese. They did the same for the British when London's East India Company (EIC) established its first trading post in India at Surat port in 1612. When the EIC headquarters moved to Bombay, large numbers of Parsis anticipated the opportunities this offered. Encouraged by the British, they quickly came to dominate trade and commerce in the growing city, and established lucrative networks overseas. Many Parsis became leading shipping agents and master shipbuilders.

It's estimated that by 1800 Parsis owned half of Bombay, including many of its most magnificent properties, some of which they leased to British rulers. Later, with industrialisation, the Parsis set up the first cotton mills in Bombay and were instrumental in founding the Indian steel industry. Alongside great wealth, many families also gained prominent roles in the public life of Bombay and Gujarat. In accordance with Zoroastrian doctrine, Parsi entrepreneurs established numerous charities and educational organisations that benefited the wider community.

Despite their small numbers Parsis today continue to play a major role in Mumbai and other parts of the world. One example is the Tata Group. Founded by a Parsi family from Navsari, the business has grown into a huge multinational company and is one of the UK's largest private sector employers. It has 45,000 UK employees working for nineteen different companies, including famous names like Tetley, who blend and sell tea, and Jaguar Land Rover.

Left: A man delivering milk outside Vadi-Dar-E-Meher temple in the Parsi neighbourhood of Navsari. Navsari is considered by Parsis to be their religious capital in India, as it contains some of the most important Fire Temples in the world.

Right: Homi Bapuji Kotwal sitting in the entrance of Vadi-Dar-E-Meher Parsi temple, built in the twelfth century. Homi has looked after the holy fires at the temples of Vadi-Dar-E-Meher and Atash Behram in Navsari for over 50 years.

Above: A Parsi priest buying vegetables near the Desai Bhagarsath, an important Parsi Fire Temple in Navsari.

Right: Muslim women in a quiet backstreet of Navsari. The house they are passing can be identified as belonging to Parsis by the symbols, which represent the Zoroastrian concept of holy fire.

25

THE SIDDI COMMUNITIES

Gujarat, the Middle East and the coast of East Africa have had a long history of trade, involving constant exchanges of goods, ideas and people for well over two thousand years. Siddis are the descendants of Africans who first arrived in Gujarat more than 400 years ago. Some came as merchants, sailors, servants and mercenaries but the vast majority were brought to the subcontinent as slaves by Arab and Portuguese merchants.

In Gujarat there are large Siddi communities living in towns and villages around the Gir Forest National Park, such as Talala and Jambur. It is believed that the Portuguese presented their ancestors as slaves to the local nawab of the nearby city of Junagadh.

These communities have largely adopted the language and culture of local people, but some African traditions have survived. The call to prayer at the mosque in Jambur is not the voice of a muezzin but the beat of a drum. Most of the estimated 20,000 to 55,000 Siddis who live in India are Muslims, although there are also small Hindu and Christian communities too. As well as Gujarati

Siddis, there are also large communities in Karnataka and Hyderabad in India and Makran and Karachi in Pakistan.

The photographs here were taken in Jambur, a village of about 500 people where virtually all the residents are of African descent, part of one of India's largest Siddi communities. It's a very poor village where people collect and sell firewood or work as labourers for neighbouring farmers. They also receive help from the government under an affirmative action programme for poor communities.

Left: Siddi men sitting on the steps of the mosque in Jambur, one of several towns in Gujarat where the majority of people are Siddis.

Right: A painting in a palace in Bhuj of an Indian nobleman smoking a hookah and surrounded by his servants, who include a trio of African boys.

Above: *A man carries a tray of burning incense during prayers at the mosque in Jambur, which houses the tomb of a saint known as Nagarchi Baba, or Drum Master.*

Right: *The mosque in Jambur.*

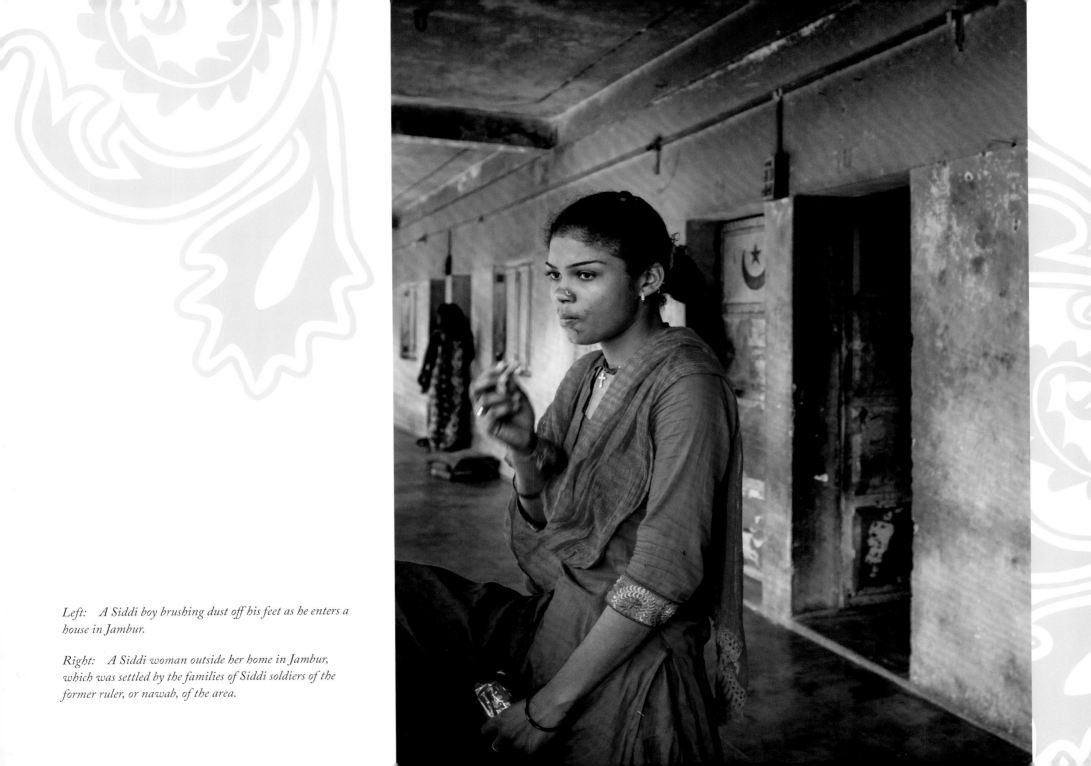

Left: A Siddi boy brushing dust off his feet as he enters a house in Jambur.

Right: A Siddi woman outside her home in Jambur, which was settled by the families of Siddi soldiers of the former ruler, or nawab, of the area.

The Arrival
of Europeans

Trade has been going on between India and Europe for thousands of years. The Europeans particularly prized spices such as cloves, nutmeg and pepper for use in food, medicines and perfumes. But these spices had to be brought overland along the ancient spice routes, a long journey which greatly increased their cost. By the fifteenth century the Europeans began looking for a direct sea route to the East.

The Portuguese were first to open up a sea route from Europe to 'the Indes'. In 1498 the Portuguese sailed around the southern tip of Africa for the first time. Guided by Gujarati navigator Kanji Malam, the Portuguese explorer Vasco da Gama went on to reach India. Aggressive and heavily armed, the Portuguese used their large merchant fleet to establish a chain of coastal trading posts stretching from East Africa right to Japan. They made huge profits from selling spices and other goods direct to European markets.

Once the cargoes reached Portugal, they were shipped to nearby countries by the Dutch merchant fleet, which was then the largest in Europe. Working

so closely with the Portuguese, the Dutch realised that they too could make huge profits from trade with the East. In 1595 the Dutch used Portuguese maps to sail to the spice islands of Indonesia, returning with a cargo of peppercorns and nutmeg. They established trading posts and a headquarters at Bantam, a major city on the Indonesian island of Java where traders from Gujarat, Arabia, Turkey, Iran, Malaysia and China met to sell their products. The Dutch and the Portuguese also had bases in India at ports such as Surat.

The eastern traders bought and sold an incredible range of goods – spices, tea, textiles, carpets, porcelain and china, drugs and gourmet foods. English merchants were eager to become part of this lucrative trade, and in 1600 London traders set up the East India Company (EIC), which was granted a royal charter by Queen Elizabeth I for exclusive trade with the East.

Just two years later the first EIC ships arrived at Bantam. In this hot tropical climate the spice merchants were not interested in the heavy woollen cloth the English had brought to sell, and as the

Dutch and Portuguese fought to control the pepper trade, the English were forced out of Indonesia. So the EIC turned its attention to India. The first EIC ships to reach India simply anchored offshore and traded with merchants already there. Many of these merchants were based in Surat, the hub of India's maritime trade and the gateway to Agra, the capital city of the Mughals who ruled much of India at this time.

The EIC wanted a territorial foothold on the subcontinent and sent representatives to the Mughal Emperor, Jahangir, seeking permission to set up a base locally. In 1612 it was agreed that in exchange for European goods, the EIC could establish its first onshore trading centre in the main Mughal port of Surat.

Instead of selling woollen fabrics, the English began to trade in Indian goods, especially Gujarati textiles, which were famous throughout Asia for their design and quality. These fabrics were exchanged for other goods, which along with Indian silks, cottons and calicoes, were taken back to London and sold at a huge profit. By 1650 there were many more EIC

trading posts dotted along the coast of India. The trading post at Bombay eventually grew to become the EIC's Indian headquarters, and the port itself became the main link between Britain and India.

By 1750, the Mughal Empire had been weakened by a series of wars and was breaking up into smaller states. The EIC took this opportunity to extend its territory in India. Moving beyond its role as a trading concern, the Company made treaties with some local kingdoms, and attacked and defeated others using its own private army. By the early 1800s the EIC had imposed its rule right across India.

Left: Children exercising outside Our Lady of the Sea, a Catholic church built by the Portuguese as part of St Jerome's Fort in Daman.

34

Above: A couple take a short cut across the battlements of St Jerome's Fort, built by the Portuguese between 1614 and 1672 to protect the town of Daman.

Left: The Dutch cemetery in Surat where wealthy families competed with each other to build the grandest tomb.

DAMAN AND DIU

Daman and Diu are 'Union Territories', areas of land independent from the surrounding state of Gujarat. Along with Goa to the south, these Union Territories were captured by the Portuguese during the sixteenth century, and remained under colonial rule until 1961. Portugal continues to give the former citizens of Union Territories automatic citizenship if families can prove that they were resident there before 1961.

The Portuguese converted many people in these territories to Roman Catholicism. The Christians of Daman and Diu use a Portuguese dialect and also speak English, Hindi and Gujarati. There are also large Christian communities in and around Mumbai who can trace their origins back to the days of the Portuguese. Although churches in Mumbai remain very busy, the congregations of the many churches in Daman and Diu are shrinking fast. Father Sebastiao Mascarenhas, the head of the Roman Catholic Church in Daman, spoke of how many people are leaving Daman and Diu for Britain.

'There is a growing sense of insecurity among the Christian community in India, and substantial numbers of people have recently left Daman, Diu and

Father Sebastiao Mascarenhas blessing a cross that is about to be erected outside the Church of Our Lady Of Remedios, one of the many Catholic churches in Daman.

Goa. There are now big communities in places like Wimbledon, Wembley and Leicester. I only had two baptisms in Daman last year, so it's a community that's going down very rapidly. In the next ten to 15 years we expect that only the old people will remain.

In Daman it's not only the Catholics who are going but also Hindus and Muslims too. If people can prove their family lived here before 1961 they are entitled to an EU passport. But they don't go to Portugal, they go to England. The language they speak here is pidgin Portuguese, Daman-style, that can't be understood in Portugal. Even I had a hard time understanding it when I arrived from Goa. But the language of education is English, so people speak English and go to England for work.

It's the unskilled jobs the British economy needs filling, so they do shelf stacking, even with good qualifications they do that kind of work for the minimum wage. That generation will struggle with poor pay and poor housing, and I've seen what it's like in England, but people go for the sake of their children, their future. They call themselves NRIs (Non-Resident Indians). But they're NRIs no longer, they're EU citizens!'

A man at prayer in the Church of Our Lady Of Remedios in Daman.

Tourists visiting the ruins of the Portuguese fort in Diu, which guarded this tiny trading island just a few hundred metres off the coast of Gujarat, until it was reclaimed by India in 1961.

39

A litter of puppies follow their mother through the heavily fortified entrance of the Portuguese fort in Diu.

Worshippers at the Feast of the Nativity of Mary, held at the Mount Mary Church in the Mumbai suburb of Bandra. This festival is part of the annual Bandra Fair which began over 300 years ago when a statue of Mother Mary, dreamt about by a local fisherman, was found floating in the Arabian Sea.

41

Catholic pilgrims make offerings of flowers in the grounds of Mount Mary Church, which attracts between 50,000 and 100,000 visitors a day during the week-long Bandra Fair.

Above: Fisherman Vinod Karssan mending nets in the port of Vanakbara on Diu Island. As a long-term resident of this former Portuguese colony, Vinod is entitled to an EU passport, for which he has applied, as he is planning to join his relatives in Wembley.

Right: A Catholic nun at Mount Mary Church in the Bandra district of Mumbai.

43

THE EAST INDIA COMPANY

The East India Company (EIC) was set up as a commercial trading company in London in 1600. It soon became an extraordinary success and can be compared to a modern multinational, but its power and reach were unique. At its height the EIC issued its own currency, ruled over a sixth of humanity, controlled half the world's trade and earned those who ran it huge fortunes. It had its own navy, the Bombay Marine, and 250,000 soldiers at its command.

EIC ships reached India in 1608 and the first EIC trading post was built in Surat in 1612. Other posts soon followed, and for 150 years the EIC operated from these coastal bases, guarded by private armies recruited in England. Mughal rule provided a convenient network for trade inland, and the EIC grew rich exporting cheap Indian goods overseas.

During the eighteenth century the English and French fought for dominance in India, and both nations recruited local Indian soldiers. Armies led by French and British officers fought on Indian soil. As the Mughal Empire declined the EIC moved beyond its role as a commercial company. It made treaties with local rulers, and defeated others

River dredgers moored on the Tapi River, Surat, at the spot where the British first came ashore in India and set up their earliest trading post.

– and the French – with its armies. By the early 1800s the Company had imposed its rule across India, setting up British courts and collecting taxes.

During the Industrial Revolution Britain needed cheap raw materials, and markets for its manufactured goods: India was used to provide both. The EIC forced Indians to sell their raw cotton cheaply and to buy back expensive cloth made in Britain. Farmers were also coerced into growing opium for the EIC, who made vast fortunes selling it for export it to China, where it was traded for tea.

Many of the policies and laws imposed by the EIC were contrary to Indian interests and culture, and there were many uprisings against it. In 1857 the Indian Mutiny or Great Uprising started when troops of the EIC's Bengal Army rebelled against their British officers. It took two years of bloody fighting to suppress the Uprising, and when British forces finally regained control there were massacres of both rebel soldiers and citizens. These events caused widespread distrust between the British and Indians. As a result of the uprising, the British government abolished the EIC, passing all its powers, property and lands to the crown. The British Raj had begun, ruling India until its independence in 1947.

The tomb of Captain George Nicholas Hardinge in St. Thomas Cathedral, the first Anglican church to be built in Bombay. Hardinge's tomb describes him as dying a 'hero's death' in a sea battle in 1808, and praises him as 'the terror of the Indian Seas'.

Military memorials in the Anglican Church of St John the Evangelist in the military garrison district of south Mumbai. Known as the 'Afghan Church,' it was built by the British to commemorate those killed when the East India Company attempted to invade Afghanistan during the nineteenth century.

Model soldiers in the Dr Bhau Daji Lad Museum in Mumbai. The East India Company ran its own private armies, made up of local men as depicted here, and commanded by British officers.

Above: Morning assembly at Rajkumar College in Rajkot. This was one of three schools in British India modelled on the British public school system, designed to educate and train the sons of Indian rulers, equipping them with the outlook and skills thought necessary for leadership in British India.

Left: The Maharaja's Palace in Bhuj. Built in the 1860s as a home for the ruler of Kutch, it was designed by a British architect using Mughal, Kutchi and European styles, and built by Italian and local craftsmen.

RAJKUMAR COLLEGE

"The representatives of the British government chose three places. Rajkumar College here in Rajkot catered for western India, Rajkumar College in Raipur catered for central and eastern India, and Aitchison College in Lahore was for the north – that's now in Pakistan. These three places were chosen to educate the princes of the ruling states and the sons of zamindars, the landlords. They could be educated in the English ways, you may say, and then be able to govern their small kingdoms on behalf of the British who needed an Indian to rule the Indians, but with the British training and thinking.

So the British started these so-called public schools where only the princes studied. They were put into hostels, they were taught all the etiquettes of messing, dining, dressing and social customs. They spoke in English, and then they appeared for the Senior Cambridge examinations. They were taught extra subjects which were not in the Indian curriculum, like agriculture, as they would be dealing with agriculturalists who paid the revenue on the land they ruled, the taxes. They taught them a bit of horse riding, and flying a plane. The school had a small Piper two-seater trainer aircraft and a glider. They were taught the best of everything. They taught them courses of law also. So you came out as a young ruler. So this is named Rajkumar College, Rajkumar means prince, the son of a ruler.

The College was started by the Britishers with the support of the rulers of this local area who donated the land and money for the buildings. The Britishers themselves first ran it, with principals appointed from England. It was to give

themselves, the British, the rulers of tomorrow who would help them to govern India. So we have a rich history of the British connection.

Many of our students have gone on to the UK. The connection of many of these rulers was with Britain only, so they chose to go to Britain. It was the most powerful country in Europe, so where else would they go? And so then automatically the majority of other people from Rajkot followed them and went to England. They went there first, the rush to go to the USA came much later. Now of course they have spread all over, and that includes many of our former students.

We have an exchange programme with UK schools and French schools. Both teachers and students go on exchange programmes. Students come from there and stay with host families for three months here in India, and then the Indian child goes to stay with those families there for three months. So that cultural interaction is there alongside the exchange of ideas.

The children of NRIs also study here. Their parents send them to relive their past, to retain the cultural heritage of their motherland. Because they are abroad sometimes they feel their culture is getting diluted so they come here to revive that culture for that next generation, and then

they will take it forward with a global thinking. The older ones might have gone abroad for economic reasons, in pursuit of income, but the current generation will go not only for income but also for cultural exchange and with a broader global mindset, but one rooted in India. It helps not only Britain but also India and the world at large."

Abijit Das, Vice Principal at Rajkumar College.

Right: Portraits of former students hang alongside those of the British Royal family in the Bhavsinhji Hall at Rajkumar College in Rajkot. The college was established in 1868 'for the education of the Princely order'.

A man pays his tailor for a new suit near Uganda Road in Porbandar. This district near the railway station is full of grand houses built by wealthy merchants when Porbandar was a busy international port.

53

The entrance to the Watson Museum in Rajkot, where a list of instructions includes the rule that 'Prohibited things are not allowed'.

Above: Books in the library at Naulakha Palace, which is still occupied by the descendants of Sir Bhagwant Singhji, but has rooms open to the public.

Left: A young girl walks through the complex of courtyards surrounding Naulakha Palace in Gondal, former home of Sir Bhagwant Singhji, ruler of the local kingdom from 1888 until his death in 1944. Singhji was educated at Rajkumar College and studied medicine at Edinburgh University and law at Oxford.

Building Bombay

Bombay was originally made up of seven islands. Over the centuries these islands were joined together to form present-day Mumbai, a city of 20 million people and the financial and business capital of India.

The original islands were home to fishing and trading communities long before the Europeans arrived. In 1534 the Portuguese bought the islands from the Sultan of Gujarat, and then gave them to King Charles II of England as part of the dowry on his marriage to Portugal's Princess Catherine in 1661. The king saw little value in these unhealthy, swampy islands and leased them to London's East India Company (EIC) for a pittance.

The south-east tip of the islands formed a natural deep-water harbour, around which the EIC built a protective fort. This area, known as Bombay, became the EIC's headquarters in India and grew rapidly, attracting traders and entrepreneurs. These included Gujaratis who had the skills, contacts and experience from working in the older commercial centres

A huge statue of a Lamassu, a protective mythical creature that marks the entrance to a Parsi fire temple on Dr Dadabhai Naoroji Road in Mumbai. The road is named after the Parsi educator and cotton merchant who became the first Indian to be elected as a British MP, representing London's Finsbury Central constituency, in 1892.

further north. Among them were many enterprising Parsi families, who established themselves as leading members of Bombay's business, administrative and industrial elites, whose descendants still live in the city today.

Some Indians worked in partnerships with the British while others set up on their own. Between them they began draining the swamps and reclaiming land from the sea. They built a thriving commercial city with busy dockyards and a ship-building industry. The EIC built up a fleet, called the Bombay Marine, which consolidated British power along the western coast of India, while the Company's private armies provided security for local residents. The city was a source of work for craftspeople and builders, and wealth for a growing middle class. In 1853 the first Indian passenger railway was opened, running 21 miles from Bombay to Thane. A year later the city's first cotton mill opened, and soon a booming textile industry added to the city's position as a major industrial and commercial centre. Many of those with influence and power became fabulously rich, and the city's importance and prosperity was reflected by its grand architecture, much of which survives to this day.

A mural on a wall surrounding the Indian Navy dockyard at Lion Gate in Mumbai.

Above: The Chhatrapati Shivaji Terminus, Mumbai's iconic railway station, which was the largest British-built edifice in India when it opened as the Victoria Terminus in 1887. The first passenger train service in India ran from here to Thane in 1853. The station now handles over three million passengers daily.

Right: Rush hour traffic outside the Oriental Life Assurance Building in south Mumbai. This area of the city was redeveloped in 1860 when the original fort built by the East India Company was demolished and replaced with grand buildings and broad avenues reflecting the city's wealth and importance.

PERCY MISTRY

"I was born in Bombay in July 1947. My mother said that I was sufficiently frightening even then for the British to leave the country within three weeks of my birth. I was one of Salman Rushdie's Midnight's Children.

My father was a member of a Parsi family who had made their money from the late 1800s right up to the end of the Second World War. My mother's family was more recent in their migration from Iran, which is where Parsis originated. Her father became the Municipal Commissioner of Bombay, the chief administrator under British rule at the time. He was one of those Parsis who, although few in number, became a thin membrane between the colonisers and the colonised, and played a very significant role in government, in business and in the armed forces. Parsis had a reputation in Gujarat for fair ethical dealings. They did not give their word easily, but when they gave it they kept it. This made them trusted by both the Indians and the British.

When you look at how few British people conquered India, that small number did a phenomenal job. They did it through divide and rule, understanding the psychology of the rivalries that occurred between the Maharajas, the Rajas, the Nazeems. The Parsis weren't the initiators

and propagators of this strategy, but they were the tacticians and implementers, through their negotiations and knowing what the British wanted and what the Indians could deliver. They were principally the people who formed that professional layer, and their influence and their presence is still way beyond their numbers.

The Gujaratis were experts in finance, and they knew the Parsi merchants very well, so there was a sort of co-migration, and Bombay became their magnet. When it became a really busy thriving port, the Parsis were the first non-British shipbuilders here. They built the first frigate for the British Indian Navy, and the clippers for the China trade. They started reclaiming land from the sea, got into real estate, and then into textiles and textile machinery, which was really important in the First and Second World Wars. People forget how much war material was being produced in India and shipped out to Europe. These were not only formative years for Bombay, they were extremely profitable years, and at that time the Parsis and the Gujaratis dominated trade and finance.

When I was born my family had assets in the UK, but we all grew up here. The buildings where we grew up were built on land reclaimed from the sea

Percy Mistry having lunch at the Cricket Club of India, near his home in Churchgate, Mumbai.

by my grandfather and his associates. The sort of Art Deco-style apartment buildings that you see in this part of Bombay [Churchgate] were built by the Parsis. My grandfather built a few and kept two; we grew up as a reasonably well off, middle-upper class family. At the time I was born my father and his brothers were heavily into the Turf Club, into horse racing and breeding. They used to go to Ascot every year, they raced horses there too.

My father had business interests in Rangoon, in Panang, in Singapore, Hong Kong, and Japan. The family also had business interests in Europe, in Lancashire textile mills, and a house in South Kensington. We always had foreign visitors at home, they were from China or Japan, or German, French and English, so it was a very cosmopolitan outlook. My life was a ball, as I'd make friends with the children of these people who came to India. I thought that was normal, that every child grew up like that!

I left for England in 1963, on Indiaman Tours, who used to run buses overland from London to Bombay. My father became a shareholder in the company when the first set of buses broke down. They were British Leyland buses and we had a British Leyland factory here, so my father had the buses refitted and in return they gave him a share of the business. I rode on the back of that and became a courier and [aged 15] went to England by road.

I went to Dulwich College and did my A-levels in London, and met my wife while doing a degree at Loughborough University. She got a job in Toronto, so I moved there to marry her and studied for my MBA and PhD. I first worked for the Ford Motor Company in Toronto and then ended up at the World Bank in 1970. After travelling and setting up a merchant bank in Hong Kong, I came back to the World Bank and fulfilled my lifetime ambition to retire at the age of forty. But I've been working ever since!

I've lived abroad since I was fifteen, and I don't know what I am any more. I'm not English or American or anything else, but I do sometimes ask myself 'How Indian am I?' I think I've become very much a creature or inhabitant of the world. I feel at home everywhere, but sometimes I worry about not feeling as much at home as I should do, when I am here in Bombay. But if I was to assess where I am today, there's as much of a British cultural influence as there is Indian. For example, it still irritates the hell out of me when I see anyone queue-jumping here!"

Staff at the Britannia and Co, a traditional 'Irani café' in the genteel Ballard Estate business district of Mumbai. There were once hundreds of these cafés, set up by Persian migrants to India during the days of the Raj, but now fewer than thirty remain.

Customers at the Yazdani Restaurant and Bakery in Mumbai. The menu and decor of this Irani café and Persian style bakery have hardly changed since it opened in 1953.

ALBERT,
PRINCE CONSORT.

Above: The Rajabai Clock Tower at the University of Mumbai, built in the Neo-Gothic style of architecture popular in nineteenth century Bombay.

Left: A statue of Prince Albert, the husband of Queen Victoria, standing in the main hall of the Dr. Bhau Daji Lad Museum in Mumbai. The Museum was opened as the Victoria and Albert Museum in 1872.

Independence

India's independence came about after a long struggle against British rule, first against the East India Company (EIC) and then against the British Raj.

From 1750 onwards the EIC functioned less as a commercial enterprise and more as a nation state. It gained power through alliances with local rulers, devious political rulings and bloody military conquest. The Company set up local governments staffed by former officials from its trading posts, establishing British courts of law and taxation to fund its massive armies. The EIC attempted to impose Western values on many aspects of Indian life and tolerated no resistance. Charles Grant, an EIC director, wrote in 1792: *'Is it not necessary to conclude that [our Asiatic territories] were given to us, not merely that we draw an annual profit from them, but that we might diffuse among their inhabitants, long sunk in darkness, vice, and misery, the light... of truth?'.*

There were frequent rebellions against this harsh and inflexible British rule, the largest being the Indian Mutiny or Great Uprising of 1857. This began when EIC troops stationed near Delhi rebelled against their British officers. The dispute was sparked off by the introduction of ammunition allegedly greased with pig or cow fat, offensive to both Muslim and Hindu soldiers, who had to bite the greasy paper coverings off the bullets before use. Of the 139,000 sepoys in the Bengal Army all but 7,796 took up arms against the British. The revolt spread rapidly, the rebels capturing Delhi and other cities. Supported by widespread civilian unrest, the Rising developed into the greatest and bloodiest revolt against a European colonial power in the nineteenth century.

When the British regained control, the British government abolished the EIC and placed India under direct rule, appointing a Viceroy on behalf of the British monarch. The Raj had begun, but hostility to British control continued undiminished. The Indian National Congress was formed in 1885, and in 1906 the All-India Muslim League was created to represent the country's Muslims. These groups campaigned at first for greater representation for Indians, and later for total independence.

Bombay was an important centre for the independence movement, and Gujarat and its people played a leading role in the nationalist struggle. The most famous figure in the struggle for self-rule was a Gujarati, Mohandas Gandhi, more commonly known as Mahatma Gandhi. Born in 1869 into a well-off merchant family in Porbandar, Gandhi studied law in London and worked as a

lawyer in South Africa. Returning to India in 1915, he began to organise widespread protests against the excessive taxes imposed by the British. In 1921 he became leader of the Indian National Congress, leading national campaigns on behalf of women and the poor, with the ultimate objective of self-rule (or Swaraj) for India.

Gandhi's campaigns emphasised nonviolence and civil disobedience. In 1930 he led the now famous Salt March, to protest against the tax levied by the British on the making of salt, from his Sabarmati Ashram in Ahmedabad to the beach at Dandi, where he made salt from seawater. His subsequent arrest and imprisonment had a profound effect on the Indian independence movement, attracting millions of new followers, and led to worldwide condemnation of British rule.

In 1939 the Second World War broke out. Without consulting any Indian leaders, the British government declared India to be at war. In response Gandhi and the Indian National Congress denounced Nazi Germany, but declared that India could not support a war supposedly being fought for democratic freedom while that freedom was denied to India. Despite this, an army of two and a

half million volunteer soldiers was raised in India, fighting under British command and playing an important role in the Allied victory.

As the war progressed calls for independence increased. In 1942 Gandhi launched the 'Quit India' movement during a speech in Bombay, calling for non-cooperation with the British until they left India. The British immediately arrested Gandhi and over 60,000 other Congress members. Key leaders were kept in prison until June 1945, although Gandhi was released in 1944 because of ill health.

Once the War finished, Indian independence became inevitable. The Partition of India in 1947 was designed to allow the British to withdraw as quickly as possible. Partition divided the old colonial state into two independent ones: India and Pakistan. The Indian National Congress, the secular but primarily Hindu-led party, assumed control of India and the Muslim League took Pakistan, the separate Muslim state for which it had campaigned.

Left: A statue of Mahatma Gandhi in Manek Chowk in Porbandar. This square is in the old city next to Gandhi's birthplace, the red building visible through the archway.

During the ten-day Ganesh Chaturthi festival virtually every street in Mumbai erects a statue of Ganesh, the Hindu elephant deity. This has been the city's most popular celebration ever since the 1880s when it became a focus for India's struggle for independence and resistance against the British, who had banned all public assemblies.

Men dressed as tigers dancing at the parade held at the end of Mumbai's Ganesh Chaturthi festival. This group are from Karnataka State in southern India and have come to the city at the invitation of the Karnataka community who live in southern Mumbai.

Above: A stilt dancer painted as a tiger takes a break from the parade that marks the end of the Ganesh Chaturthi festival.

Left: Families on Chowpatty beach, one of the many beaches in Mumbai where, at the end of the Ganesh Chaturthi festival, statues of Ganesh are immersed in the sea.

Above and left: Visitors to Dandi Beach near Navsari. Dandi is famous as the place where Gandhi made salt at the end of the 240-mile Salt March from Ahmedabad, protesting against taxes imposed by the British. When Gandhi was jailed for making his own salt it drew worldwide attention to the Indian independence movement and sparked large-scale dissent in India, leading to the imprisonment of over 80,000 Indian protestors.

Above: The statues erected by the British at key locations in colonial Bombay are now stored in the gardens of the Dr Bhau Daji Lad Museum. Attacked as symbols of British rule, they were moved to the Museum for safekeeping. They include several figures of Queen Victoria, this one with her nose hacked off.

Right: The Mumbai skyline from the Oval Maidan, a park in the south of the city. The three landmarks from left to right are the High Court of Bombay, the Bombay Stock Exchange and the University of Mumbai.

The Leopold Café in the Colaba area of Mumbai is one of the city's oldest and most famous restaurants, established by Parsis in 1871.

Lawyers walk past a cow tethered outside Watson's Hotel in Mumbai's legal district. The hotel was the most prestigious in the city during the colonial era.

Passengers wait for a train in Morbi, one of India's 7,172 railway stations. India has one of the world's largest railway networks, carrying over eight billion passengers annually and employing over a million people.

A woman dressed in the distinctive fashion of Mumbai's Bohra Muslim community, carrying a child outside a second-hand shop in the Do Tanki district of the city. The variety of goods and music on sale reflects the city's cosmopolitan mix of people.

A horse and jockey after a race at Mahalaxmi Race Course in Mumbai. The course has hosted horse racing since 1883 and is home to the exclusive Royal Western India Turf Club, which advertises itself as 'an exclusive Club enjoying the patronage of socialites and eminent personalities alike'.

Spectators gathered around the parade ring discuss the runners and riders before a race at the Mahalaxmi Race Course.

Above: A promotional film for India's new football league being filmed in Horniman Circle, originally built as the financial centre of British-era Bombay. The Indian Super League was launched in 2014 and became an instant success in its first season, with crowds averaging 24,000 people attending matches across the country.

Left: Taking afternoon tea in front of the main pavilion at the Cricket Club of India in Churchgate, Mumbai. Built on land reclaimed from the sea, the stadium attracts big crowds for its high-profile cricket matches. One of India's most prestigious sports clubs, it is also a meeting point for members of Mumbai's business and social elites.

Above: *Willingdon Crescent, a shopping arcade overlooking the busy bazaar of Chelmsford Market in Jamnagar. The arcade was commissioned by Maharaja Sir Ranjitsinhji Vibhaji who was inspired by his travels to Britain where he attended Cambridge University. Between 1896 and 1902 he played cricket for England and became famous as one of their greatest ever players.*

Right: *Early morning yoga outside the Baroda Museum & Picture Gallery in the Sayaji Baug in Vadodara. The park, its buildings and its extraordinary art collection featuring work by British painters including Constable and Turner, were all donated to the city by Maharaja Sayajirao III, who ruled Baroda State from 1875 to 1939.*

Journeys to Britain

Indians have been coming to Britain for nearly 400 years. The first to arrive here were sailors, and the ayahs (nannies) and servants of British families returning from India. Next came a small number of professionals - mainly doctors, businessmen or lawyers – who established themselves in Britain from the mid-nineteenth century onwards. The majority of Indians arrived after 1945 when Britain faced a shortage of labour and recruited people from overseas, usually from places that already had strong colonial links with Britain.

It was partly because of these colonial links that Gujaratis became the largest group of migrants to come to the UK from India. Gujarat's position as the ancient centre of an international trading network meant that many of its people were accustomed to looking overseas for new opportunities. They were sailors, traders and entrepreneurs with broad horizons and long traditions of travel and migration. When they heard about the labour shortage in Britain, many of them had the confidence to make the move. Single men arrived first, and once they found work, they would look for jobs for their male relatives and friends back in India. As the UK communities became more established their wives and children joined them.

Bombay was another important link between Gujarat and Britain. The city may have been ruled over by the British until 1947, but it was largely Gujarati businessmen, traders and workers who built and ran the city. They had the contacts and the resources to make migration to Britain relatively simple for themselves and fellow Gujaratis.

The booming port of Bombay also attracted people seeking work from other parts of the subcontinent. Many men found employment in the docks, and then as sailors on British merchant ships, especially stokers who shovelled coal into the furnaces of coal-fired steamships. When these seamen returned home to their towns and villages in Gujarat and what is now modern-day Pakistan, they would recruit other men to join the British fleet.

Bombay also played a vital role during the First World War, when 1.3 million Indian troops were involved, and during the Second World War, when 2.5 million Indians constituted the largest volunteer force in the world. Many of these troops travelled through Bombay on their way to fight in Europe. Some of the veterans of these conflicts then went on to settle in Britain and it was they, alongside former merchant seamen living in dockland areas, who laid the foundations of Britain's early Asian communities.

East Africa was another link between Gujarat and Britain. India had established a trading empire in Africa long before the British went there, and

Gujarati traders were already active in most of East Africa's coastal cities. As the British made their way into East Africa building roads, railways and trading posts, a huge Indian workforce went with them. The British recruited the engineers and skilled workers, mainly Gujarati and Punjabi, who had worked with them on roads and railways back in India. Many of these workers settled in East Africa, and went on to establish very successful businesses in construction and engineering. It was these East African Asians who were forced out of their homes by newly independent African states in the 1960s and 70s. Because they were British passport holders, many of them came to the UK rather than going back to India, a country which some of them had never visited.

As a result, family networks that stretched between East Africa and Gujarat have sometimes been brought together within a single neighbourhood of a British town or city. Ties with India have not been lost, but are maintained by visits to family, by marriages, and by investment in land, property and businesses. Many places in both Britain and Gujarat have been transformed by the process of migration and settlement, and will remain linked by it for generations to come.

Left: A street trader in Navsari sitting below a statue of Dadabhai Naoroji. Born into a family of local Parsis, Naoroji was the first Indian to become a British MP, representing Finsbury Central constituency from 1892 to 1895.

A collection of family photographs belonging to Manu Mistry who, along with his parents, has lived his life in Navsari while the rest of his family emigrated to Africa, Fiji, the USA and Britain.

A boat builder in Diu scrolls through photos of his friends and family who have moved to live in London.

The ICICI bank in Rajkot advertising its services to NRIs, or Non-Resident Indians, who live abroad. Advertisements aimed at NRIs are very common on banks and billboards across Gujarat, particularly in towns with strong overseas links.

Pratima and Subhash Sampat, who live in Harrow near London, shopping in Mandvi during a visit to their ancestral home in Kutch.

Above: *Derelict houses in Alipore, which belong to people who now live abroad. The first big migrations from Alipore were to South Africa and East Africa, and then from Africa many people moved to Britain.*

Right: *New houses next to the doctor's surgery in the village of Karadi, close to Dandi beach near Navsari. Like many other large houses in the area, these belong to NRIs who return on holiday, and remain empty most of the year.*

LAXMAN RAGHWANI

Laxman and Prembai Raghwani at their home in Baladia near Bhuj.

"I was born here in this village, Baladia, in 1930. My father died when I was only six months old. We were two brothers and a sister and a very poor family, my mother had a cow and sold the milk. I started work when I was nine years old, weeding on a farm. But there was little work here so people started to go to Kenya. I borrowed the money for the fare and in 1947 I left from Porbandar with 50 or 60 people, on a dhow to Mombasa. Then I went to Nairobi and started masonry work, carpentry, and I started learning. I didn't have any engineering degrees or anything but in 1953 I started my company in Kenya and we got ourselves a good name. So we start working in the Seychelles, in Mauritius, and then in Bombay and Ahmedabad.

When we started in 1953 we were working with the British Government, building office blocks, bungalows, hospitals, shopping centres. Then many people from our community in Kenya, Uganda, Tanzania, Zambia and Malawi went to the UK, because after independence in these countries they wanted to give work to African people and make life difficult for us. We were never Kenyan citizens, we had a British passport, and they wouldn't give us a work permit.

So in 1965 we took our money and we start a business in the UK. We'd buy the land, and build and sell the flats and houses, and construct hospitals and such places. When we started we had about twenty people and slowly, slowly we built a big company. Today we have about 300 people in England, about 1,000 people in Kenya and about 200 people in India. A few of the people we employ in London are from Baladia, with many people from Diu and Daman. And running the businesses, I have one son in Kenya and two sons in London.

When I left Baladia in 1947 it was a small place, very poor, mostly mud houses. This house was built of mud. Today it's very different. It's a big village with big houses built with money from London, most of our community are in London. But these doors in this house are the old doors from our mud house, 120 years old; my father built these doors with his own hands.

People from our community were carpenters and stonemasons mostly, but these days many people are going into industry, import and export, hardware and sanitary businesses. And people are studying now, being doctors. Before you couldn't study, no one here could even read English, there was no telephone or telegraph. I used to make my signature with my thumb, but then when I was in Nairobi I was working in the day and I would study at night. These days I spend two months in London, July and August, and the rest of the year divided between Nairobi and here."

The Apna Ghar Home for the elderly in Madhapur, near Bhuj. The costs of building and running this centre are met by the residents' younger relatives who are living abroad.

MUHAMMED GARDA

"I've just arrived from England this morning. We've still got to get unpacked. A couple of our suitcases are full of supermarket food, so the family here can try it. When the British came to India, they went back with the Koh-i-Noor diamond. And look at what we bring back in return, packets of Pringles!

My dad had a BA degree here, an education, but when he went over to England it counted for nothing. He worked in a carpet mill in Batley, and then when the mills closed down he got a job in Leicester and we moved there.

I was born in Dewsbury and I married a girl from Gujarat, so I come back here regularly. Work only allows me three weeks off, but I come back every couple of years. It's an education to bring my kids here. They've seen it on TV but it's important to see it for real. At this age they remember everything and they get to meet the grandparents. If we don't keep ties with family back here we don't know where we came from, and what hardships the family went through to get where we are today."

Left: Groceries bought in Leicester.

Right: Ahmad, Huzaifa and Aadil, three brothers on a family holiday from Highfields in Leicester, get a lift from their uncle to a wedding party in Lajpur, the village from which their grandparents emigrated during the 1970s.

Friends from Brighton and London take pictures at an ancient step-well in Adalaj near Ahmedabad. 'Normally when we come here it's just to see family, or for a wedding. But this time we've made some time for ourselves and we're doing a tour and seeing the sights.'

An NRI riding a brand new motorbike chats to local friends while on holiday in Lajpur.

LEENA MISTRY

"I was born in Leicester in 1983. My father was sixteen when he moved to England, my mum was eleven and they migrated from Kenya in the early '70s. My father's family came one by one, when they could afford it. He came on his own and was taken in by friends of the family. The same happened with my mother's side. [My parents] didn't know each other in Kenya, but they married in England. Originally my father's side of the family is from a small village just outside Navsari, and my grandfather migrated to East Africa. He owned a small store. On my mother's side, her father worked in a bank in Nairobi, and when he came to England he struggled, as he just couldn't do factory work.

I grew up in Loughborough. We had the Indian upbringing at home, but step out of the house and it was western culture. My father was a chartered accountant in a small village nearby where he definitely felt his ethnicity, and worked just that extra bit harder to prove himself. When I was young there weren't many Indian families, but my father wanted us to adapt. European languages were encouraged, western classical music was encouraged. I did Grade 8 piano, and me and my two sisters were the only Indians who played in the county orchestra. We lived in a very white neighbourhood, and [my father] felt that if he

could incorporate all these activities, that would help us integrate; and they did help us. Music, learning French, our holidays were always cultural holidays. We couldn't just go to Spain and lie on the beach! We had to learn about Spanish culture.

Most people I was playing with in the orchestra went to music school. I did have the choice to go, but you know, that Indian thing about choosing a profession came in so I did a law degree in Sheffield. I first came to India on a legal project in 2006. When I finally moved it was a point in my life where I didn't want to get caught up in the rat-race. I'd established friends over here and they said 'Oh, you should come over here and teach music, you'll love it here'. Teach? I thought nobody wanted to learn piano in India, they'll want to learn Indian instruments. But people said 'No, no, there's this new market that's booming and you'll really fit in'. Within the Christian and Parsi communities, western music has been part of their culture for centuries. So I did my research and slowly people started coming, and now I have a regular set of students.

It's through music that I feel I can integrate wherever I am, and I feel I'm offering more than just music in my lessons. OK, we may have a McDonalds around the corner, but this is a way for my students to learn about a foreign culture

through music, which takes commitment, and a lot of people want their children to study abroad. Like it helped me integrate into society it could do the same for them.

For my parents and grandparents generation India was a place they left because they didn't have the opportunities they hoped for, that's why they left. For them England has provided them with the opportunities to succeed. So they think it's going to be a struggle over here. But the place has changed so much, it's a very different world today. It's difficult to explain over the phone to those who migrated a long time ago, who are holding onto a culture that existed decades ago. Parts of it still do exist over here, but people here are not holding onto that. I don't know if it's always progression, but here they're moving on.

A lot of NRIs come to India on holiday, and most of them do the standard thing; go back to Gujarat and go back to the village. They've changed a bit, those places, but not that much. You need to come to a place like Bombay to be at the forefront, to see what new things are really happening over here. It's a very exciting time to be in India. Things are moving all the time, so quickly. Being part of that environment really makes you think about what you're doing and make the most of life. Instead of living in a small sleepy town and letting things

pass you by. But it does take a certain character to want to be part of that. If you want to make things happen you feel like you can make them happen over here, I think may be that time has been and gone in England.

It's not necessarily all new ideas, but taking things that have worked in England and applying them over here. It's in a different context, which makes it interesting and very challenging. It's not plain sailing, but that's what makes it very exciting."

Leena Mistry on the seafront near her home in the Bandra district of Mumbai.

SANTA HIRANI

"I was born in Nairobi in July '58. My grandfather
travelled [to Africa] from Baladia to work on his
own farm, growing vegetables and fruit. My father
worked in a bank in Nairobi. But when I was three
I came back to India and I grew up in Baladia. I was
here for sixteen years and then we went to England.
I went in 1977, on a flight from Bombay to London.
Oh my God, it was very different to what I was used
to in a village. But I arrived on a Friday and on the
next Monday I started work in a factory making
glasses, in Wembley. There were 70 or 80 Gujarati
people who worked there. My brother-in-law, who
was a supervisor, got me the job.

It was very easy, but after four years my children
came so I left there and was I working as a dinner
lady, and doing cleaning jobs. Part time, so I can
look after my children. So I'd get up at four o'clock,
go to work cleaning, and come back to drop my
children at school. And then at twelve o'clock I start
as a dinner lady, and then when I finish that I cook

*Devshi and Santa Hirani talking to another visitor at the
Mahadev Temple in Baladia near Bhuj. They both spent
most of their working lives in Brent, Devshi working as a
builder and Santa as a school dinner lady, and have retired
and returned to the town where they grew up.*

and clean and look after my children. It was a hard life, a really hard life. But my headmaster was very nice, and he arranged that in the holidays I would look after the children of some of the mothers who were working, running a creche. It was a Catholic primary school. I would go to the temple in Ealing Road because I am a Hindu, but sometimes I would also go to the church. I would see the children and the mums, and it was 'Hello Santa', 'Hello Santa', everyone would be very friendly.

Now we are back in Kutch to look after my husband's mum. The first plan was, we would look after her in England, but she doesn't like England, especially the cold weather. She doesn't speak English; she can't even catch a bus so how can she go to the temple? All the time she was crying so we came back here. We've been here four years, and I miss England and I miss my daughters, but one day I will go back to live in England."

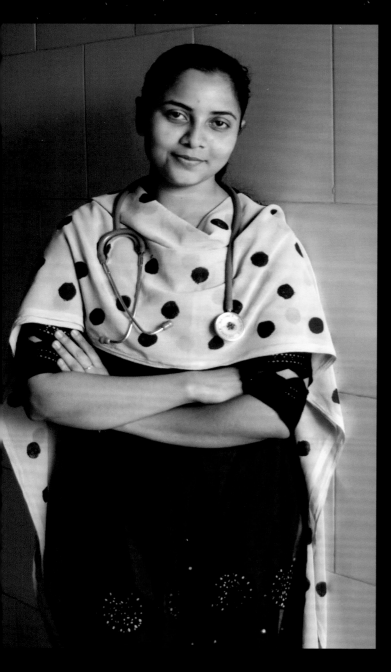

ALIPORE HOSPITAL

"My father moved from Alipore to Bombay in 1937, where he ran a medical store. So he did well and he acquired a vast knowledge of medicine, and he was the inspiration behind opening this hospital. He came from a poor background, but he said it would be this work that would speak for our family.

We started running a clinic in 1994 and then opened a four-bed nursing home. This was such a success we had the ambition of building this hospital with 125 beds. Half of the construction costs came from the family, with the rest as donations made locally and from the UK. Considering the low economic status of the people in and around Alipore, the hospital is run mostly on a charitable basis.

Every other home in Alipore has a connection with the UK. People went from here to labour as textile workers in Manchester, Blackburn, Batley and Bradford, and they have settled in London and Leicester too. We receive major donations from Alipore people in the UK, as well as organisations, like Muslim Aid UK, which have no connection with Alipore.

We provide a service here for everyone, regardless of caste or religion. When you're doing charitable work you have to concentrate on serving people, you have no option but to serve them whoever they are."

Hassan Mayet, President of Alipore Social Welfare Trust.

Left: Dr Mahefuz Vakkus on duty at Alipore Hospital, which provides medical services for local people whatever their income. Much of the money needed to build and run the hospital is donated by NRIs living in Britain.

Right: Rafik Mulla, a taxi driver from Dewsbury, has flown from Britain to visit his father who is recovering from a sudden illness in Alipore Hospital.

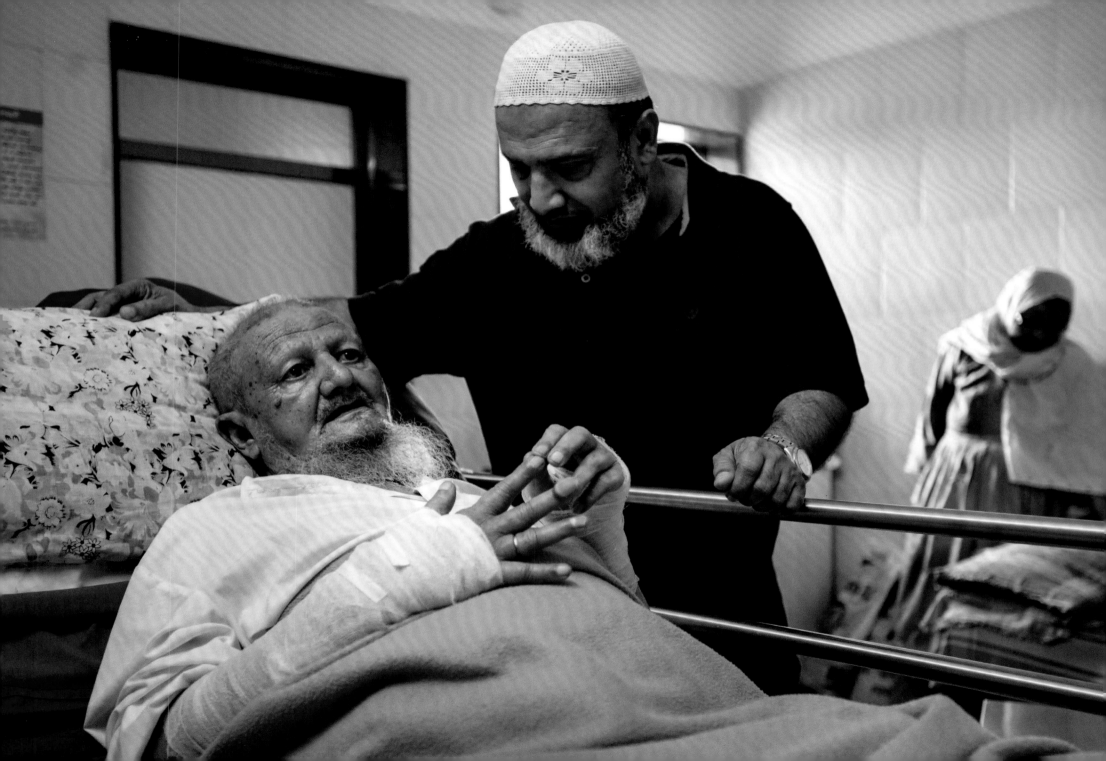

The Sanatan Seva Mandal school and orphanage in Dwarka provides an education for 435 students whose parents can't afford government schools. Around half the students, many of them orphans, are resident at the school, and a significant part of the money that supports them is donated by NRIs.

A boy eating breakfast at the Sanatan Seva Mandal school.

Left: Girls trampolining at the Munshi & Dadi Patel English Medium High School in Lajpur, which was established by families who are now living in the Dewsbury area of Yorkshire.

Above: A cricket match outside the Shree Ghanashyam Academy. This English speaking school near Bhuj was set up with the support of Swaminarayan communities in Gujarat itself, as well as those in Britain, North America, Africa and Australia.

NARAN BHUDIA

"Madhapur people are very broadminded. They were the first to go to Africa, the first to go on to the UK. You name it, they went there. Then people like my great grandfather from Sukhpar [near Madhapur in Kutch] followed them. They all went in small boats from ports like Jamnagar and Mandvi, and settled along the coast of Africa, and to Muscat [in Oman] too. It took one month on a sailboat, sometimes longer depending on the wind. Then when the steamers arrived it took ten to twelve days. I went in 1954, from Bombay to Mombasa, twelve days on a big steamer. 'State of Bombay' was the name of the ship. Everybody flies there these days.

I lived in East Africa until the 1970s and then we all had to move to England. Us Sukhpar people will tend to settle in one place abroad, like there's lots of us in and around Brent. But the Madhapur people will go anywhere. London, Leicester, Cardiff, Birmingham, Oldham, you name it. They're all over England."

Naran Bhudia at his home in Sukhpur, near Madhapur. Most of the men who emigrated from this area were from the building and carpentry communities who had worked with the British building the railways in Kutch, and then moved to East Africa to do similar work.

GULAM ISHMAIL

"I'm from Pipaldara, where there are many people, about 25 houses, of the Khalifa community. In the old days our main job was cutting hair. Now people do different jobs: some are farmers, some are agricultural labourers with sugar cane, some are weavers and some still cut hair. They commute to the town nearby, Gandevi, where they have barber shops. There's also a textile factory in Gandevi where many people work.

It was my father who went to Mombasa to work on the East African Railways. He worked there for twenty years, but after Kenyan independence they put Africans in our place and we all lost our jobs. I was about 30 years old and we came back to India. But we had British passports from Kenya, and in 1966 I went to Bradford, which is where I've lived ever since.

I started work straight away with British Rail, and worked for them for 30 years. In East African Railways I was a clerk, but in Bradford I worked as a ticket collector and as a platform guard at Bradford Interchange and Forster Square, and in Keighley, Shipley, Bingley, Saltaire and Halifax. I retired in 1994."

Gulam Ishmail, who divides his time as a pensioner between Bradford and Pipaldara near Surat.

GULAB PATEL

"I was born in 1934. Before independence this area around Eru Char Rasta [in Navsari] was very different, it was all farms, but since then all this area has been developed. Now there are a lot of people from overseas and there is a lot of income. When they went from the villages to the foreign countries they got the money to make the buildings over here. In the beginning they would buy the land and build it themselves but now they buy from a developer. Lots of people here come and go. Between November and March most of the NRIs [Non-Resident Indians] come over here from UK, Australia, America and Canada. But most of the year our street is quite empty.

Navsari has changed in every way. Before, in the old houses, there were no facilities at all. No toilets, no bathrooms, no water or electricity. Now everybody has a nice house, with water, gas, electricity. They've got everything now, a fridge, car, motorcycle. So many things.

This is my motherland, so I try to come every year. We meet our relatives; we do some charity work installing water pumps in rural areas, and in schools who work with the blind and disabled. And we enjoy a holiday.

A man pressing sugarcane at a juice stall in Valsad.

So many people from my village went to Africa. In my family my father was the first to go abroad. First of all he went to Mombasa, and then he lived in Uganda. He was a construction worker and then he had a small building firm. Then my brother and I went, but my mother never went further than Bombay. Their aim was just to earn some money, come back and develop something here.

I went to Uganda in 1949 when I was fourteen and left in '67. I was working in an insurance company and got two months' holiday. A few friends of mine were living in England and they used to talk about it, and so I thought I'd go to see how it was. My brother-in-law was in Bradford so we had no choice, we went to Bradford. My first job was as a bus conductor. Then I got a job in a factory making machinery, Croft's Engineering, and I ended up making tractors at International Harvester.

In the beginning we had a lot of difficulties because I went with the whole family, my wife and five children, and we got just one room to start with. It was the month of May, 1967. There were already many Gujaratis there, and if you saw anybody you'd have a talk with them. But it was difficult to meet people because there was only one Gujarati Samaj [association]. But nowadays there are a lot of temples, samaj, and so on. Each and every one has their own organisation."

Gulab Patel and his daughter Vismita from Bradford at their favourite sugarcane juice stall near their home in Navsari, where they often stay during the British winter months.

114

Left: Jessica and Owen, a couple from Wembley, at a ceremony to bless their forthcoming marriage at a Hindu temple in Gadat, held before their return to London for their English wedding. The family of the bride are originally from this area near Navsari, and have returned to celebrate with relatives living locally.

Above: A graduate of Edinburgh University poses for photographs with his new bride at a wedding in Ahmedabad.

The family and friends of the groom make their way to his marriage ceremony in a noisy procession through the streets of Navsari.

117

The groom and his party dance in the streets of Navsari on the way to his marriage ceremony.

Gujarat Today

Gujarat has a long history of commerce and relative prosperity, and this is reflected in its current status as one of India's richest and most developed states. From the 1960s onwards Gujarat state followed a policy of rapid industrialisation and increased agricultural output. In farming this meant a change from subsistence to cash crops, with irrigation projects and subsidised electricity for farmers. The government invested in heavy industry, petroleum refineries and chemicals.

As a result Gujarat state is home to some of India's biggest cement, chemical and pharmaceutical manufacturers, huge oil refineries and a thriving textile industry. The government has also encouraged smaller industries through land release and tax breaks. However services such as transport, housing and water supply have struggled to keep pace with this rapid growth, and industrialisation has also brought serious environmental problems alongside severe water shortages and droughts.

Urban areas have expanded very rapidly, many villages becoming industrial townships with a tangled mix of roads, houses, shopping malls, factories, temples, and mosques all competing for space. The state has some of India's largest and fastest growing cities, such as Ahmedabad (5.5 million people) and Surat (4.4 million people). The ancient centres of these cities are being redeveloped and the

surrounding suburbs growing at an extraordinary speed. There are still strong links between particular cities and industries: textiles and car manufacturing in Ahmedabad, textiles and diamond polishing in Surat, petrochemicals in Vadodara, and engineering and machine tools in Rajkot.

Gujarat now has one of the highest per capita incomes in the country, attracting large numbers of migrant workers from the rest of India, who come hoping for well-paid jobs and a higher standard of living. There is however a growing gap between the rich and the poor, and many workers, especially these migrants, are still living below the poverty line.

The entrepreneurial spirit is thriving in Gujarat, with a fast growing middle class, and booming markets in land, property and retail. Over half of Britain's direct investment in India goes to Gujarat state, and the region is important in the relationship between the two countries.

Investment in the state has been boosted by the many Gujarati NRIs (Non-Resident Indians) around the world who fund businesses and other projects in their ancestral towns and villages. Some people do question the rapid pace of development, however, such as this British-born woman whose parents came from Surat: *'My mother and father often go back to the place where they grew up. But what was there then, and the India that they are attached to, is rapidly disappearing. It does bring into question what they go back for.'*

Left: Apartment blocks being built on farmland in the rapidly expanding suburbs of the Pal Gam district of Surat.

Above: Sugar cane, one of Gujarat's main crops, on sale in Ahmedabad.

Right: Processing sugar cane at the Valsad Sugar Factory. The factory is run as a co-operative, with over 16,000 farmers who are members and shareholders. Most of these farmers are smallholders who farm just a few acres of sugar cane.

Left: New houses and offices being built on farmland surrounding Surat. The huge demand for land in and around Gujarat's expanding towns and cities is encouraging local farmers to sell their land and establish themselves in other areas, although this is becoming more difficult as the price of land rises across the region.

Above: Unloading food products into a warehouse in Vadtal. Over 60% of Gujarat's population live in rural areas and depend on agriculture and associated industries to make a living.

ABDULHAI GARDA

"In British times this town (Sachin, near Surat) was capital of Sachin state, ruled by a nawab. In the eighteenth century people from this district went to South Africa. They went by boat. They were farmers and they went to cut sugar cane in South Africa, and some went to do the same in Fiji, to find a better future.

It was later they went from here to England. In 1950 some big families went to the UK and then they sponsored their relatives. I was at university here, doing a literature degree, and when I'd finished my education I went to England. My wife to be had gone with her parents, and then I went in '78 to get married. I started working in a carpet factory in Birstall near Bradford as a machine operative. But my two brothers were in Leicester so I got a job there in a leisurewear factory making jeans. There's a big community from Lajpur in Leicester, and also in Dewsbury and London, areas like Hackney and Leytonstone.

Nowadays I'm a pensioner, and I come back to India every year. Before when I was working it was every five years, to visit family. I come when it's English

Abdulhai Garda of Leicester surveys the river running through the village of Lajpur where he would go swimming as a child.

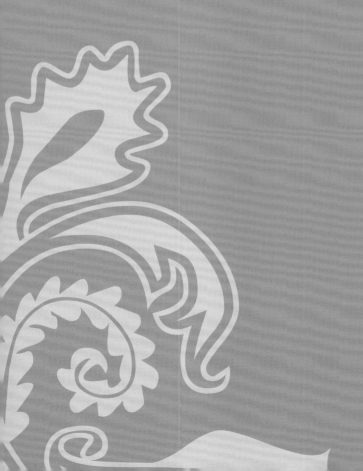

wintertime. It's better when it's cooler here. In the summer, March to July, it's burning hot. Too hot!

When we were kids we would come swimming at this spot. There used to be fish, birds, peacocks even. Beautiful! But now look at it, the water's all black and oily from the industry upstream."

Diamond polishing at Finestar Jewellery & Diamonds in Surat, where an estimated 92% of the world's diamonds are cut and polished before they are exported back to diamond trading centres in Antwerp, New York, London and the Middle East. The trade has created nearly 500,000 jobs in Surat, and attracted migrant workers from other parts of Gujarat.

Above: The Birla Cement Factory in Porbandar. Much of the traditional architecture in Gujarat's rapidly growing towns is being replaced with modern concrete, glass and chrome buildings.

Right: New hotels and offices being built on the site of demolished textile mills in central Surat. As the value of land in the centre of the city increases much of Surat's manufacturing industry is moving to the outskirts of the city.

SEWA

The Self Employed Women's Association (SEWA) began in Gujarat in 1972 when a group of poor, illiterate women working as casual labourers in Ahmedabad's wholesale textile markets came together to form a trade union for self-employed women. SEWA, which is based in Ahmedabad, now has over a million members in Gujarat, and around two million in the rest of India.

While around 94% of India's female labour force still lacks union representation, women in SEWA have been able to improve their incomes and working conditions through collective action. The organisation provides a range of services to working women, including affordable banking, training, and access to healthcare and education.

SEWA plays a particularly active role in Gujarat's booming construction industry. In Ahmedabad alone they have 30,000 members working on building projects, with 75 women working on the development pictured here. Traditionally women have been employed as casual labourers, earning a daily wage of between 200 - 250 rupees [between £2 - £2.50]. SEWA has been training women to enable them to work in skilled trades, such as plastering

A member of SEWA, the Self Employed Women's Association, working as a plasterer in Ahmedabad.

and bricklaying, which enable them to earn between 400 - 450 rupees per day. SEWA also provide a range of support services: negotiating monthly contracts between women and construction companies who often hire workers on a casual daily basis; monitoring prompt payment of wages; providing health and safety training and equipment, and organising group insurance for the workplace.

SEWA commented: '*Our movement is enhanced by being a sangam, a confluence, of three movements: the labour movement, the cooperative movement and the women's movement. With globalisation, liberalisation and other economic changes, there are both new opportunities as well as threats to some traditional areas of employment.*

More than ever, our members are ready to face the winds of change. They know that they must organise to build their own strength and to meet challenges. There are still millions of women who remain in poverty and are exploited despite their long hours of hard labour. Women bear the brunt of the changes in our country and must be brought into the mainstream, so they can access the new opportunities that are developing with regard to employment.'

Members of SEWA working as bricklayers on an office and retail development in central Ahmedabad.

Men using smart phones on the promenade at Dwarka.

Mobile network adverts outside electrical shops in Valsad.

A poster of the Hindu deity Hanuman in a café in Adalaj, near Ahmedabad.

A new shopping centre in Ahmedabad, one of many opening across the city to cater to the rapidly growing middle classes.

Textiles

I ndian textiles have been prized for their beauty and quality since ancient times, when they were traded in markets from the Roman Empire in the west to China and Indonesia in the east. The Gujarat region played a pivotal role in the Indian textile trade, producing textiles and providing the main ports through which the cloth was exported overseas. Gujarati textiles have been influential within India itself and throughout the world, from Indonesian villages to the great houses of the European aristocracy.

When the Europeans arrived in India they bought Gujarati cloth in order to barter it for spices in Indonesia. But they also brought the cloth back to markets in Europe, where it became very fashionable, particularly in England.

The East India Company (EIC) began selling Indian cloth in London in 1613. By the 1670s, the EIC had moved away from selling spices to supplying Indian textiles to the home market. These textiles had a profound effect on British furnishings, dress and design. The Company developed new styles, which it thought would appeal to western tastes, and sent out patterns for Indian weavers to copy. These designs evolved into hybrids, combining elements of western, Indian and later East Asian textiles.

It was cotton textiles that dominated Britain's early trade with India, with silk and other fabrics playing a lesser role. The EIC made huge profits partly through the sheer quantity of fabric it sold. But it also rigged the trade, forcing Gujarati and Bengali weavers to work exclusively for the Company, and using its armies to ensure that they complied.

The EIC's export of textiles from India peaked towards the end of the eighteenth century. By the mid-nineteenth century the flow of goods was reversed, with Britain becoming the dominant exporter of textiles. The Industrial Revolution had brought new technology, power and machinery, which transformed the production of textiles in Britain. Manchester became the world's first industrial city, combining new technologies with factory production systems to make it the centre of the British cotton industry. Gujarati spinning, weaving and printing techniques that had been carried out by hand were industrialised and could be done much faster in the mills. Britain began to flood world markets with mass-produced cloth, including copies of Indian textiles.

Gujarati hand weavers were unable to compete with imported fabrics on price or quality and could only maintain a market for very rough cloth or very fine specialised goods. At the same time, the British imposed high tariffs on Indian textiles and restricted their export. India was forced to sell raw cotton cheaply to Britain and to buy expensive yarns and fabrics in return. India responded by industrialising its own textile industry. The first cotton mills were built in Bombay and Ahmedabad in the late 1850s. Although the British had rigged the trade to favour British producers, these mills went on to establish large domestic markets for their goods.

Despite this, the amount of cloth woven in India fell by 40% between 1850 and 1880. The plight of Indian textile workers was a catalyst for the rise of the 'Swadeshi' movement, which encouraged Indians to boycott British imports and played a vital role in the struggle for Independence.

In the 1950s and 60s, Britain experienced a labour shortage and recruited thousands of textile workers from South Asia to work in mills in Manchester, Yorkshire, Lancashire and the Midlands. It was this call for labour that attracted many Gujaratis, eventually making them the largest group of Indians to settle in Britain. Experienced textile workers went to places like Dewsbury, Batley, Bradford and Blackburn, where they could use their skills and experience. Others relied on their connections in Gujarat and Mumbai to establish import and retail businesses as part of the flourishing trade that supplies textiles to Asian communities across Britain.

During the early 1980s large-scale textile manufacturing in Britain went into dramatic decline and has now virtually disappeared. Production has transferred to areas with cheaper labour elsewhere in the world. Some of it has shifted back to India, and Gujarat's textile industry is thriving once more.

Left: Premji Hari Manvar, who works from his home in the weaving community of Hamapur near Junagadh. The domestic manufacture of textiles from locally grown cotton is an age-old industry that supports most households in his village.

Above: *A family picking cotton on their farm in Virpur, near Gondal. Cotton is one of the most important crops in Gujarat, which produces more of it than any other state in India.*

Left: *A shepherd leads a flock of newly-shorn sheep through Lajpur. Gujarat's textile industries are based mainly on cotton, but wool is also an important raw material for manufacturing finished goods.*

Above: *Deliveries of cotton to a ginning factory near Gondal where raw seed cotton is processed. The seed cotton goes through dryers and cleaning machines that remove dirt, stems and leaves, before circular saws with small, sharp teeth pluck the valuable fibre from the seed.*

Right: *A family in Virpur returning home for breakfast carrying sacks full of cotton picked in the cool hours of early morning.*

Above: Sweeping up at a factory near Gondal, where cotton seeds are processed for by-products such as cottonseed oil and cattle feed.

Right: Hand spinning using a charkha, a spinning wheel powered by hand, at the Udyog Bharti Khadi centre in Gondal.

KHADI — LIVERY OF FREEDOM

When Britain began mass-producing woven cloth during the Industrial Revolution, this had a huge impact on the textile industry in India. The British imposed high export tariffs on Indian cloth and forced India to sell its raw cotton cheaply to English mills in cities such as Manchester. Indian textile production declined by 40% between 1850 and 1880, the workforce experienced great hardship, and the country became reliant on expensive imported cloth.

Indians responded with a movement that became known as 'Swadeshi' or self-sufficiency. Swadeshi had two aims: to protest against British rule by boycotting British products, and to strengthen the Indian economy by buying Indian products. 'It is difficult to measure the harm that Manchester has done to us' Mahatma Gandhi stated. He argued that 'Foreign cloth must be totally banished from the Indian market… Protection of [India's] staple industry is her birthright'.

Khadi, a handspun, handwoven cloth made from cotton, silk or wool, became a powerful symbol of Indian nationalism and resistance. Gandhi was often photographed with his 'charkha,' a spinning wheel used to spin the yarn for khadi cloth. He described the traditional cotton dhoti and shawl that he wore as the 'Livery of Freedom', because they were made from yarn that he'd spun himself. The production of khadi cloth demonstrated Gandhian ideas in action, inspiring millions of people and helping to fuel the struggle for independence from Britain.

Khadi cloth continues to be produced today, particularly in Gujarat. Demand currently outstrips supply, as the cloth has become popular with India's emerging middle classes. There are now over 5,000 organisations promoting Khadi as an alternative to large-scale industrial production, providing employment for millions of people in towns and villages across India. Khadi continues to be a symbol of freedom, and a traditional product that embraces contemporary designs and ideas.

Left: A woman weighing yarn at Udyog Bharti, an organisation in Gondal which supports over 2,000 spinners and weavers producing Khadi. The organisation supplies them with raw materials and markets and distributes their finished products.

Right: Preparing spun yarn for weaving at the Khadi centre in Gondal.

Kanku Manvar preparing yarn for weaving on her veranda in Bagasara. This village has a large number of families who work from home, many of them making denim. Their output is collected by local Khadi groups who distribute it to larger organisations in the cities, where much of it is used to make jeans for well-known brands such as Levis.

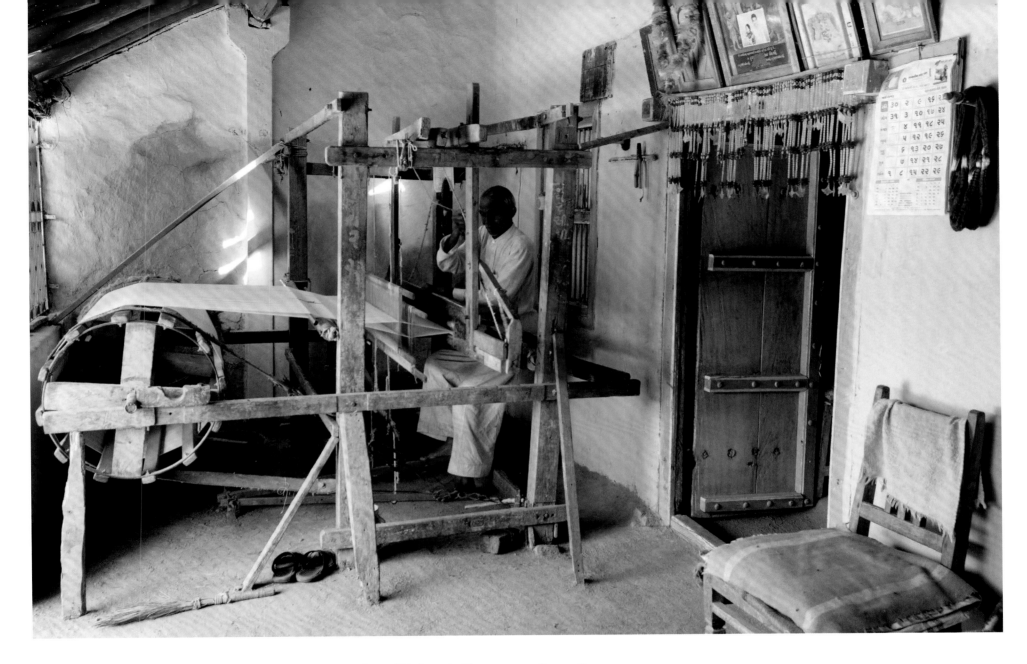

Premji Hari Manvar at work on a loom in a room built onto the front of his house in Hamapur near Junagadh.

146

Above: *A weaver at work in the Katargam Darwaja district of Surat.*

Left: *A weaver watching over his looms in a backstreet weaving shop near the railway station in Surat. Thousands of the city's textile workers are employed in small units such as these, where both working conditions and rates of pay are very poor.*

Workers inspecting cloth at Garden Vareli Mills in Surat, the largest manufacturer of sarees in India. The company uses both cotton and synthetic materials to produce cloth for the domestic and export markets.

Preparing silk screens for printing at Garden Vareli Mills. The tens of thousands of different designs produced here reflect both the rich textile traditions of India and contemporary influences from all over the world.

Overleaf: Preparing colours in the dyeworks and inspecting sarees as they emerge from a silk screen printing machine at Garden Vareli Mills in Surat.

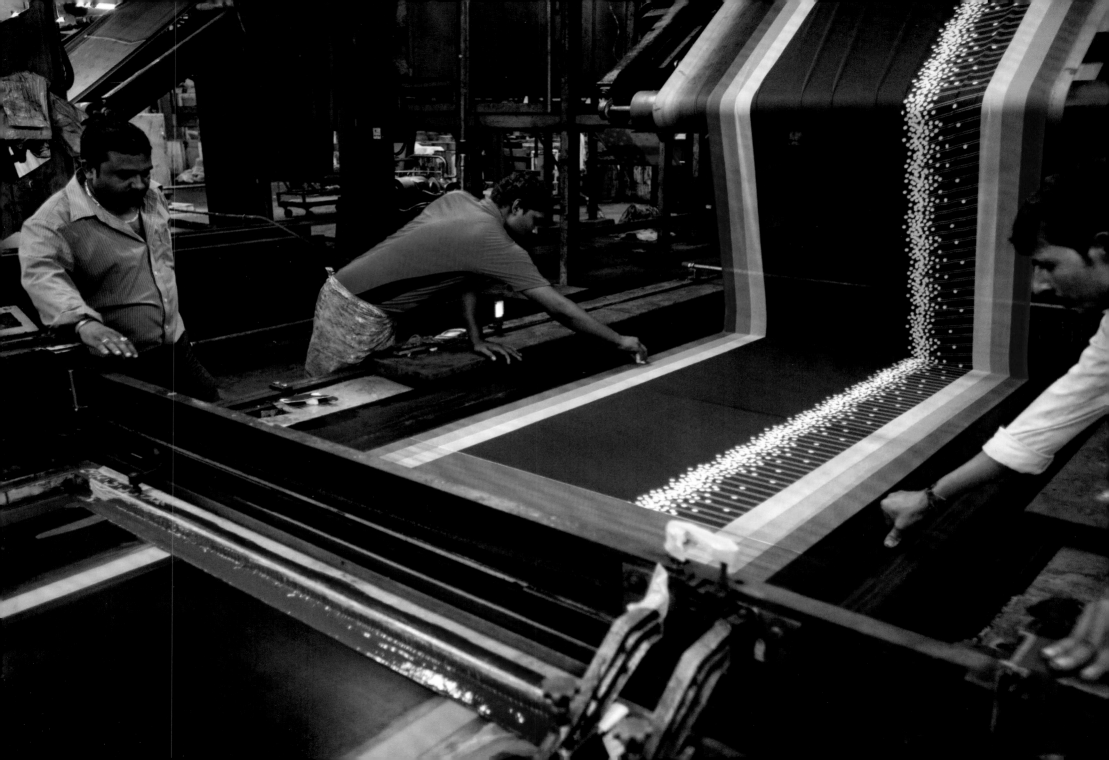

Cloth being carried to and fro amid the busy textile markets in Surat city centre.

Finished cloth being packed for sale to Indian and export customers in Surat.

Above: Women choosing saree lengths in the Old Bombay Market in Surat. This covered complex with hundreds of shops attracts customers from across Gujarat. It's particularly popular with NRIs, or Non-Resident Indians, returning to India to visit friends and family and do their shopping for the forthcoming wedding season.

Right: Porters with bales of textiles outside the Dwarkadhish Mandir on Kalbadevi Road, at the centre of the main textile trading district in Mumbai. The Mandir was commissioned in 1875 by Seth Mulji Jetha, one of Bombay's largest cloth traders at that time. Although textile manufacturing has now moved from Mumbai to Gujarat, the city's international connections mean that it remains a busy trading centre for finished textiles.

Gujarati Food

Gujarat's position on a trading crossroads means that over hundreds of years the region's food and cooking have fused together many different influences.

Some foods that are now regarded as distinctively Indian originally came from elsewhere – such as idlis [steamed dumplings] from Indonesia, samosas from Central Asia and tea from China. Various styles of cooking arrived in Gujarat with the different communities who settled in the area. The Mughals introduced breads such as naans and chapattis, the tandoor oven and meat-based cuisine. Their method of preserving ice in underground chambers was crucial to the development of the great Indian ice cream, kulfi.

Gujarati traders were exchanging foodstuffs with Europeans as far back as Roman times. Although the sixteenth century Portuguese traders mostly brought goods back from India, they also introduced a huge range of new foodstuffs to the subcontinent. Often these were foods from the Americas, such as sweetcorn, chillies, and the potato, which is still known in Gujarat by its Portuguese name 'batata'. Other Portuguese imports include the tomato, papaya, pineapple, guava, avocado, tapioca, kidney

A woman making roti at the Sanatan Seva Mandal school and orphanage in Dwarka.

beans, peanuts and cashew nuts. Compared to this cornucopia, the British brought little in terms of food to India: indeed most of the food exchange went the other way.

The landscapes and people of Gujarat are very diverse and their food culture is enlivened by distinctive regional nuances. However one thing that could be said to unite all Gujaratis is a love of good food. These days they aren't the only ones: Gujarati cuisine is now enjoyed all over the world.

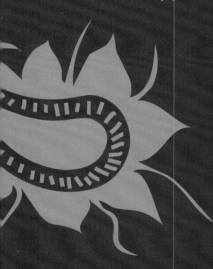

A woman buying food from a street stall outside the Shroff Bazaar in Bhuj. This colonial era building was erected by the British to house troops but is now used as a vegetable market.

KAUSHY PATEL

'Until I was four I lived with my family in a village called Ganesh Sisodra, close to my grandparents' farm in Pardi, near Valsad. There were always lots of visitors to our home, and it was through them that my father was offered an opportunity to start a business in East Africa.

We were all excited, but my grandma was worried too. Trying to settle in a foreign land with a young family would be difficult and she suggested that I be left behind with her, since we already had a special bond. Although this was true I was devastated when my mother agreed. I cried for weeks after my family left and I'd moved to Pardi to live with my grandparents. As it turned out the next ten years would be the best of my childhood.

My grandma was always cooking. At dawn she'd pick vegetables and prepare ingredients for the 'big cook' – huge pots of food for the hundred or so workers on the farm. I was fascinated by this, got involved and soon learned that I loved to cook. My grandma was thrilled and taught me until, at the age of seven, I took over cooking for the family while she cooked for the workers.

My mother arranged for me to become engaged to her best friend's son – my soulmate, Mohan.

Kaushy Patel at work in her kitchen.

So it was that I landed at Manchester airport in October 1966, not speaking a word of English, and stayed with my uncle in Loughborough while I settled in. I couldn't believe how cold and dark England was, and how early the sun set! In 1968 Mohan came to England and we married and moved up to Bradford. The Indian community was just developing and we had regular get-togethers, each of us cooking our favourite meals. I also loved cooking for my growing family, and scarcely a weekend went by without having guests to feed.

Mohan built up a reputable garage business, but by the early 1990s he wanted to do something different. Knowing that cooking was my lifelong passion, he asked whether I fancied trying the food business. A family friend was selling his launderette, which my mechanical genius husband could run, and attached was a small vegetarian deli… What could be better? My eldest son Bobby came up with the name Prashad, meaning blessed food, which seemed the perfect choice.

I got busy cooking. The deli was packed with my specialities – dhokra, kamree, pethis – and everything you would expect in a Gujarati home could now be bought at Prashad. As the years went by and the business thrived Bobby noticed that our customers were looking for somewhere they could come to enjoy a whole meal. Mohan and I knew little about running a restaurant but we introduced some tables and chairs into the deli to see how things went. Around the same time I was encouraged to enter a local cooking competition, and to my enormous delight I won! Restaurant critics came to eat in our deli-café and wrote wonderful things about our food. Prashad's reputation started to grow.

Then, in 2010, we were selected for Gordon Ramsay's Best Restaurant series. We were excited and worried at the same time. Would Gordon think we were good enough, or should we be doing things differently? Mohan was the voice of reason: he told us to stop panicking and just do what we'd been doing for years. It was business as usual and that's what got us to the competition final. The restaurant's popularity surged and as a result the deli had to close. It was a sad day for me, but since then many wonderful opportunities have opened up: opening our new restaurant and writing cookbooks. We are so happy that we can showcase Gujarati culture in our cuisine and our family ethos – we live together, and we work together and we're thrilled to share our world through our food.'

The India's Gateway exhibition and book are the result of three years of collaboration between artists, communities and staff at museums, galleries and libraries across the UK.

We would like to thank everyone who shared their time and thoughts and welcomed us into their homes and communities. We're especially grateful to those who agreed to be photographed, filmed and interviewed.

Particular thanks are due to:

Mumbai: Percy Mistry, Katie Engineer, Leena Mistry, Atul Loke, Nilesh and staff at the Abode Hotel, Alan Tweedie, Eric Rego, Yogesh Gaikwad of the Society of Dyers and Colourists, Rajeev Pai and Raju John of Bittu Cars.

Gujarat: Durgesh Jadeja and staff of Udyog Bharti, Gondal. Ramesh Vaghasia of the NRG Centre, Surat. Mashuda Shaikh, Baleshwar. Manali Shah, Geeta Koshti, and Varsha Thakar of SEWA, Ahmedabad. Abdullatif Sonara, Pramod Jethi and Naran Bhudia, Bhuj. Devshi and Santa Hirani, Baladia. Hassan Ishmail Mayet and staff of the Alipore Hospital and Research Centre. Hemant Mistry and Manu Mistry, Chikhli. Sebastiao Mascarenhas, Daman. Ambadan Rohadiya and Balwant Jani of Saurashtra University, Rajkot.

Swami Keshawanand and staff of the Sanatan Seva School, Dwarka. Balu Lad, Pravin Tailor and family, Navsari. Abdulhai Garda and family, Lajpur.

Yorkshire: Ayub Laher, Balu Lad, Ella Chavda, Mohan Patel, Kantilal Mistry, Ishwarlal Chauhan, Kala Chauhan, Bruce Cole, Steve McCabe, Dipak Patel, Ambelal Patel, Pranav Patel, Gulab Patel and family, Zahida Hussain, Abbas and Laifa Ishmail and members of The Kenya Heritage Project, Dipak Mistry, Andrew Filarowski and staff of the Society of Dyers and Colourists, members of the Noor-ul-Islam Mosque, Ahmad Lunat and the Gujarati Writers Forum, Bhagu Mistry and members of the Anand Milan Centre, Natwarlal Taylor, Narendra Mistry and members of the Shree Prajapati Samaj, Cilla Champaneria and members of the Kashatraya Sudharak Mandel, and The Friends Who Care Trust who hosted our meetings in Bradford.

Lancashire: Ishmail Hasham, Raman Mistry, Ben Pearson, Muhommad Patel, Rehmat Hasham, Ishwer Tailor, Charu Ainsworth, Ashok Chudasama, Joginder Bhamra and Charan Bhamra.

Leicester: Asha Nathwani, Piyush Joshi and members of the Belgrave Neighbourhood Centre, Hashim Karim, Kajal Patel, Madhu Thakrar, Harish Rathod, Frankie Dobara, Dahya Patel

and members of the Mandhata Senior Citizen Social and Lunch Club.

London: Derek Smith, Vardana Patel, Firoza Pathan, Bina Gandhi and staff at Ealing Road Library, Darshana Sheth and staff at Harlesden Library, Jagdish Patel and members of the Brent Indian Association, Vallabh Patel and members of the Brent Elders Group, the Redbridge Gujarati Welfare Association, Subhash and Pratima Sampat, Ajay Jobanputra, Jocelyn Bain Hogg.

Staff at the seven venues who supported the bid to Arts Council England's Strategic Touring Fund and who worked on the tour: Brent Museum and Archives, Leicester Arts and Museums Service, University of Bradford, Bradford Museums & Galleries, Kirklees Museums & Galleries, Redbridge Museum, and Blackburn Museum and Art Gallery.

Ralph Dartford of Arts Council England.

Mohan, Kaushy, Minal and Bobby Patel of Prashad, Yorkshire's award winning Gujarati restaurant, who are acting as our sponsors.

Right: An elderly man resting in Momaymora, near Bhuj.

Overleaf: A street sweeper in Porbandar.

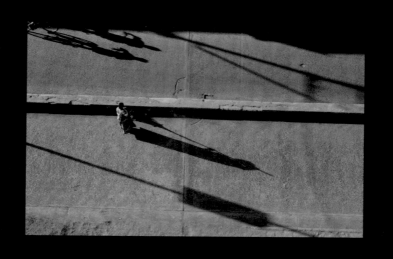